"*Be Happier Starting Now* is a gem. Combining thorough research, wisdom of the ages and personal insight, Dr. Sahelian's kind and affirming approach to happiness will surely have you glowing with a smile."
Maria Armoudian, founder, Global Network News.

"Your book is beautiful and much needed for the world we live in."
Heather Aston, Santa Cruz, CA.

"The gentle wording, natural progression of topics and evocative prose make this book inviting, supportive, practical and nurturing. The integration of physical and psychological aspects of happiness emphasizes a wise, comprehensive approach to optimizing personal and professional fulfillment. In a word, this book is *divine*."
Andrea Avruskin, physical therapist, Torrance, CA.

"You want to be happy? Read this book!"
Robert Butterworth, PhD, media psychologist, Los Angeles, CA.

"Lucid and refreshing. A pleasure to read."
Michael Gilbert, President, Albert Hofmann Foundation.

"A month has passed and I'm still enjoying your book. I even broke down and put smiley stickers around the house. I think of you with a smile when I open my front door, the medicine cabinet, the refrigerator..."
M. Holmes, software engineer, San Francisco, CA.

"I loved it. Your poetry is one-of-a-kind. Mail me twenty copies."
Jerry Manoukian, MD, Mountain View, CA.

"Our lives can be filled to overflowing with joyful, peaceful, vigorous happiness, if only we act with self-control informed by wisdom. Dr. Sahelian's delightful, well-rounded book lyrically delves into that wisdom— wisdom that we often forget in the rush of daily life. This book is gentle and soothing; we sense the author's strong sense of benevolence. *Be Happier* flows remarkably smoothly, informs broadly, and encourages us to renew our appreciation of the preciousness and glory of our lives."
Max More, Extropy Institute, Marina Del Rey, CA.

"I read. I reread. Then I read again. Every carefully chosen word, every beautiful sentence, every poetic passage teases my imagination, moves me, touches me, comforts me…"
Cassie Pham, Toastmaster, Singles by the Sea, El Segundo, CA.

"*Be Happier Starting Now* is a beautifully written book that takes a complete approach to improving happiness and the overall quality of life. Its clear style makes even the more technical sections remarkably understandable. It is full of fascinating insights into the links between health and emotions… filled with an abundance of practical, easy to follow advice. Just reading this book made me happier. I highly recommend it."
Iain Poole, Perceptions *magazine.*

"Your book is unique. Right after I finished reading it, I scanned through the pages. There were highlighted sentences on practically ever page!"
Nancy Sampson, M.S.W., Long Island, NY.

"As a family doctor I've treated thousands of patients. I often find that a patient's illness is either due to or aggravated by mental stress. Dr. Sahelian has thoroughly researched the latest scientific literature on the connection between emotions and health. He presents his findings in a warm and easily readable manner, including many practical and positive tips. *Be Happier* is an excellent book and I highly recommend it."
David Schechter, MD, Clinical Assistant Professor, Department of Family Medicine, University of Southern California School of Medicine, Los Angeles, CA.

"Thanks to Dr. Sahelian for going beyond what is taught in medical school to help us feel good about being alive."
Suzanne Taylor, Mighty Companions.

"Thoughts, emotions, left brain, right brain, body, mind, poetry, science, love, me, you, everyone, planet Earth, the universe. You put it all together. Unbelievable!"
Charles Telerman, PhD, philosopher, Boston, Mass.

"Thank you for taking me on a re-awakening journey of re-discovering myself. Your writings and thoughts are so genuine and warm that I feel I've made two brand new best friends– me… and you."
Eileen Terry, executive producer, Tony Kay Films, Inc., Hollywood, CA.

Be Happier
Starting
Now

The Complete Mind-Body Guide
To Becoming Your Best

Ray Sahelian, M.D.

Be Happier Starting Now
A Medical Doctor Explores the Fascinating Field of Happiness

Published by   Be Happier Press ♡
                   P. O. Box 12619
                   Marina Del Rey, CA 90295

Printed in the United States of America
Desktop Publishing by TMS/Russell Kurtz, PhD, RussTMS@lamg.com
Diagram page 10 by Nancie Clark, nancc@netcom.com

Sahelian, Ray
    Be happier starting now: the complete mind-body guide to becoming your
    best/Ray Sahelian.

    p. cm.
    Includes bibliographical references and index.
    LCCN: 93-092796
    ISBN 0-9639755-6-0
1. Happiness. 2. Self-actualization. 3. Self-help techniques. I. Title.

BF575.H27.R39 1995   158.1
                                            QBI94-2118

Warning– Disclaimer
The author and publisher shall have neither liability, nor responsibility, to
anyone with respect to any loss or damage caused, or alleged to be caused,
directly or indirectly by the information contained in this book.

The world would be
a better place
if more people
were happier.

Dedicated

to my brother, Ara, who, at a tender age of six months, while happily playing in his crib, became an unwilling host to a polio virus that forever robbed him of his muscle strength– but could not rob him of his will to survive. What followed were years of physical therapy, the ordeal of crutches, full-length leg braces and back braces. At age twelve, with the resolute emotional support of mother and father, he endured back surgery necessitating a yearlong hospital stay with a cast from his chest to his knees. Despite years of hardships and the daily struggle of ambulating with weak muscles against the force of gravity, he maintained a positive spirit. At twenty-three, having completed a degree in engineering, Ara moved on his own from Philadelphia to Los Angeles to survive independently, while still on crutches and braces. His *I will not give up against any odds* outlook has been a motivating example for many who have made his acquaintance. After working a few years as an engineer, Ara enrolled in night school to be a lawyer and help those who have a just cause. In the meantime he married a wonderful woman, Shelly, and together they created a daughter, darling little Allegra. On November 25, 1993, the whole family celebrated his passing the bar exam. Throughout all the years of growing up together Ara has not complained about his ordeals; moreover he has tried to motivate others to *become your best–* and *be happy– with what you have.*

Yes, there *are* extraordinary people. You may be one (or know someone) who has experienced enormous hardships, physical handicaps, or suffered life's other cruel treatments, yet have guided yourself to a satisfying life. I offer you my sincere respect, love, and admiration.

Ray Sahelian

About the Author

   Ray Sahelian, MD, is a physician certified by the American Board of Family Practice. He received an undergraduate degree in nutrition and completed his health training at Thomas Jefferson medical school in Philadelphia. Following graduation he worked for three years as a resident in family medicine where he was exposed to all aspects of medical care, including pediatrics, cardiology, obstetrics, oncology, and surgery. He was also medical advisor to a psychiatric hospital. Soon after residency he began cruising for two years in the Caribbean and Hawaii as a ship's doctor, hosting evening dinners with patrons from around the world.

   As a result of his various professional and personal experiences, Dr. Sahelian has observed human nature in tens of thousands of encounters– from birth to the grave, illness to health, calamity to success. This extensive exposure has given him profound insights.

   Traveling is one of his passions, including camping and bicycling trips. He visits at least one different country each year. Peru– hiking the Inca trail to the misty peaks of Machu Pichu– was his most recent exploration.

   In addition to his medical practice, Dr. Sahelian writes articles for newspapers and magazines, gives lectures on sleep, nutrition, and happiness, and is a frequent guest on radio and television. He genuinely wishes to share with you his practical 'it really works' approach to a fulfilling life.

Acknowledgements

I sincerely wish to thank you for your support and wise counsel.

Cindy Begel, Marina Del Rey; *Peter Doghramji, PhD*, Havertown, PA; *Bill Drucher, MD*, Marina Del Rey, CA; *Jim Farned*, Summerland, CA; *Audrey Sacco*, Santa Monica, CA.

A special thank you to

Matthew Brenner, University of California, Santa Cruz, who thoughtfully edited, revised, edited... and then some.

Steve Fechner, Hermosa Beach, CA, for practical macroadvice that influenced the course of the whole project.

Lou Mancano, MD, Norristown, PA, for sage and steady support.

Author's Note

It is possible for all of us to be happier and more loving; to savor a more meaningful existence; and to lead a life beyond 'ordinary.'

Like life itself, this book is an organic process. Reminded of Hamlet's observation to his friend, "There are more things in heaven and earth Horatio, than are dreamt of in your philosophy," I consider this book to be a maturing process and therefore would appreciate feedback from you. You may wish to write me with questions, suggestions, or simply to share your thoughts and feelings.

My endeavor has been to synthesize the wisdom of science, medicine, philosophy, psychology, history, literature, and various other disciplines, by incorporating my own personal and professional experiences. The result is in your hands.

May reading this book have a positive influence on you, and in turn, encourage you to have a positive influence on others– *creating happy ripples* that grow, spread… and return.

Ray Sahelian, M.D.

Contents

No man can reveal to you aught but that which already
Lies half asleep in the dawning of your knowledge.

The Prophet, by Khalil Gibran (1882-1931)

Overview

You can be happier than you are now.
Life can be even more wonderful.

A chef learns about condiments, food combinations, and the ideal temperature for heating particular foods, and starts cooking. A violinist learns about musical notation and how to bow the strings of a violin, and starts playing. Improving our mood and being our best can also be learned.

The big picture

What is it we're all after? Our basic motivation as human beings is not only to survive, but to be as happy as possible. Each of us tries to be happier the best way we know how– and as well as we can. Every action we take in life is done with the intention to eventually make us feel better.

There is a wide range of paths that we choose to be happier. While one person may think pursuit of pleasure is the answer, another may believe a commitment to helping others is best. Most of us lead lives somewhere between these two poles. We seek to satisfy our needs and wants, and help others when we can.

What is happiness?

In our culture happiness is often thought of as the joyful feeling that comes from having a good time or the thrill of being 'in love.' True happiness is much more than just these pleasurable feelings. It is the serenity that permeates us when we are profoundly at peace with ourselves. It is the spiritual contentment that fulfills us when we feel connected with people, nature, and more. It is the security that calms us when our financial needs have been met. It is the energetic drive associated with the passionate pursuit of meaningful goals and the satisfaction that comes from achieving them. Happiness is that overall bubbling feeling that all is well and that it's great to be alive!

As you can see, happiness includes many types of positive moods.

What is the secret to happiness?

No single path to happiness applies to every person in this world. Each person needs to find the formula that suits him or her best. Every one of us has unique genes, childhood influences, and adult experiences. But despite our uniqueness, there are ten essentials to being happier that we all share in common. Each of these is discussed as a chapter. For a quick outline see the table of contents.

Our happiness depends on how well these ten essentials are met in our lives. Conscious effort may be necessary for fulfilling some of them. For instance, achieving goals and financial security often require the postponement of short-term pleasure gratification.

The more we satisfy the essentials discussed in the following ten chapters, the more likely we are to achieve and maintain the many types of positive moods that lead to long-term happiness. Some essentials may take time to satisfy.

The ten essentials are essential

Elvis Presley and Marilyn Monroe both achieved a much sought after state of celebrity. They had legions of screaming admirers, enormous wealth, and the capacity to satisfy any type of worldly desire. In their later years they found happiness to be elusive. An essential ingredient was missing. Was it a lack of self-love or the inability to self-guide?

An artist totally immersed in creating a painting but who has no steady earnings may find, in due time, the landlord knocking on the door for the overdue rent. If financial matters have been relegated to the background, the artist may soon be soberly reminded of reality as the easel and half-completed masterpiece are transported to the sidewalk. It's harder to be creative and happy without a roof over one's head.

A workaholic may be financially secure, own an *I've won the rat race* country estate, cruise the latest model Mercedes-Benz and have a contented *honey, I love you, don't forget dinner tonight at the country club* home life. But if all this has been achieved at the expense of physical neglect– an office clouded by continuously-lighted cigarette smoke haze; rush-rush third cup of coffee, sweaty palms *hold-on, I have another phone call* at breathless pace; two-pound steak followed by double-chocolate-black-forest-cake topped with caramel-fudge-swirl *let's toast this deal, waiter, one more martini...make that two,* business luncheon feasts; *once I retire I'll relax and start an exercise program–* only to have a prosperous career prematurely disrupted by the body-can-take-so-much-abuse... *et voilà* stroke or heart attack.

Sometimes neglecting *even one* essential can disrupt equilibrium.

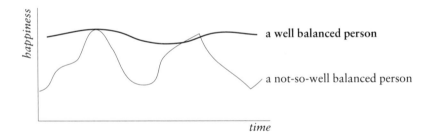

Does happiness stay constant?
Like all emotions or states of mind, happiness fluctuates. Each of us at some time in our lives experiences nature's dark storms where winds and waves buffet our boats against rocks. Hardships are an inevitable part of life's journey. Our loved ones may die or have a serious illness. We ourselves may become ill, unemployed, or a victim of a natural disaster. Anchoring our boats in a safe harbor and maintaining a constant happy state is not always possible. Life can sometimes be very difficult.

The balance beam of life broadens as more and more of these essentials are met. As we nurture self-esteem, cultivate loving relationships, pursue meaningful goals, and improve our health, we become less affected by life's surprises. Although we may grieve when visited by tragedy, hardships may also be considered opportunities for inner growth. Well balanced individuals often accommodate to difficult situations as an ocean buoy effortlessly adapts to billows and tides without sinking.

Biorhythms influence our moods as well. These biorhythms include circadian, menstrual, and seasonal.

Circadian rhythms refer to the daily sleep-wake cycle. Sleep disturbance profoundly affects mood. Circadian rhythms (or ultradian rhythms) also refer to changes throughout the day in body temperature, blood sugar, blood pressure, and energy. These changes are due to the cyclical release of chemicals and hormones by glands such as the pituitary. For no apparent reason at certain times of the day we may feel tired, sleepy, or in a low mood. A good approach to dealing with these times is just to accept them. They will pass. The cyclical release of some chemicals and hormones occurs every few hours. Try an experiment on yourself. With your right thumb press on your right nostril and close it. Breathe from your left nostril. Release your right thumb and now press and close your left nostril with your left thumb. Breathe from your right nostril. Most people will notice that air goes in one side of the nose easier than the other. In one or two hours try this experiment again. You may notice the other side is now more open. This opening and closing of the nose canals is one simple example of the changes that are constantly occurring in our bodies without our awareness.

Menstrual rhythms occur on a monthly cycle and in some women mood alterations are common a few days before a period. Fluctuations in hormones such as estrogen and progestogen cause brain chemical changes which influence mood.

Seasonal affective disorder (SAD) significantly disturbs 5 – 10% of the population during the period from October to March when days are shortest. This is due to the lack of adequate sunlight. Up to 90% of the population may be mildly affected. The symptoms include sadness,

4

fatigue, and weight gain. SAD particularly afflicts those living in northern latitudes. Women are affected more than men and the disorder is less common in those over age forty.

Some individuals are little touched by these biorhythms while others are quite significantly impaired. Biorhythm-induced mood swings are lessened by leading a well balanced lifestyle.

Do happy people live longer?

Yes. Happiness influences health and longevity. Those who lead low-stress lives, have healthy personalities, loving relationships, satisfying work, harbor few hostilities, and keep mentally active, will live longer. They will reap the following specific health benefits:

- A better functioning immune system resulting in fewer colds, flu, or other infectious diseases.
- Reduced rate of cardiovascular disorders such as heart attacks, strokes, and hypertension.
- A probable lower incidence of cancer and longer survival if stricken.
- Reduced vulnerability to various illnesses such as muscle aches, headaches, fatigue, irritable bowel syndrome, and others.

Over the last few decades scientific evidence has accumulated that undeniably supports the mind-body link. The mind (thoughts, emotions, consciousness) communicates with the body, just as the body communicates with the mind. Our moods affect the health of our body. The health of our body in turn affects our moods.

The pathways of mind-body communication are through the bloodstream, hormones, nerves, and immune system. You can find a detailed explanation of these interactions in the appendix. For now, I'll provide some brief examples. I often see many patients with flu symptoms who go through a period of mild depression for a few days. This is due to the release of substances called lymphokines into the bloodstream by the immune system. While lymphokines fight off the flu virus they travel to the brain and interfere with its chemistry, causing tiredness and low mood.

Research has shown that positive moods enhance the immune system. When subjects are shown a motivational film that stimulates feelings of caring and love, their immune system promptly improves. Negative mood states such as chronic anger and hostility weaken the immune system.

The web of life

The following is one of the most important messages of this book. *Happiness, health, personality, and all aspects of our life are connected.* They all influence and are in turn influenced by each other.

Personality is defined as *a distinctive pattern of thinking, feeling and behaving that determines each person's unique method of relating to the environment.* Personality encompasses many traits. Some of these traits include self-guidance, self-esteem, temperament (shy, extroverted; impulsive, cautious), beliefs and attitudes (liberal, conservative; optimistic, pessimistic), leisure interests (sports, music, travel), adaptability, etc. Our personality influences everything we do.

Personality has an enormous impact on longevity. Studies show that common factors shared by centenarians (those living over 100 years) are optimism, having a sense of purpose in life, and the ability to easily adapt to external circumstances. All these factors have to do with personality. Of course, we cannot deny the importance of genetics on health and longevity.

Personality is shaped by childhood and adult experiences. Personality, especially temperament, is additionally influenced by genetics. We're not a *tabula rasa* (blank tablet) at birth. Identical twins raised in different households from birth show many similarities in personality. Even though genetics and life experiences have molded us into what we are now, we still have the ability to self-guide. Through my personal and professional experiences I have observed that many people improve themselves if provided with appropriate information and motivation. Not everyone changes immediately. Ideas are seeds that sometimes take months or even years to sprout.

6

Michael is a good example. This 44 year old lawyer came in with high blood pressure and a two-pack a day smoking habit. During his first visit I suggested various beneficial lifestyle changes he could undertake to live healthier and prevent the need for high blood pressure medicines. He was not interested. I saw him regularly every three months to monitor his blood pressure and refill his medicines.

A year and a half later he surprised me, "Doctor, I remember what you talked to me about on my first visit. I'm now ready to treat my body with more respect." He followed most of my suggestions. He quit smoking, began to engage in physical activity, changed his diet to low-fat, lost weight and became more energetic. Eventually he no longer required blood pressure medications. His personality improved. Losing weight and exercising boosted his self-esteem, so his social relationships improved. He began to make friends more easily. Through his widening social circle he made many new business contacts. His income grew and he expanded his law firm. He took more time off to rest and travel. His attitudes changed– no longer was he completely dominated by self-interest at the expense of other people's welfare. Practically everything in his life improved, and continues to improve. Michael is now a happier person and continues to become his best.

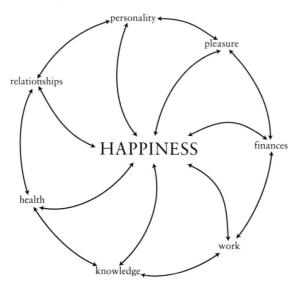

This story demonstrates the interconnectedness of health, happiness, personality, and lifestyle. The preceding diagram illustrates this point. Arrows indicate influence. This wheel of happiness is not meant to be comprehensive but simply to provide an overview.

What are some characteristics of happy people?

They are forgiving and magnanimous, optimistic, and generous in overlooking minor insults or criticisms. They focus on the positive aspects of people and circumstances. Negative thoughts such as anger or revenge are realized to be disruptive and rarely disturb their tranquil state.

Truly happy and rational individuals are unlikely to judge others by race, age, attractiveness, disability, sex, or sexual orientation. They accept those whose views differ from their own so long as no harm is done or rights are abused. The urge to act snobbishly or flaunt contentment is foreign to the person who understands that being happy means having nothing to prove. The joy of life is shared generously, and best of all there are no strings attached. Love is given from an inner abundance without a demand for reciprocation.

Our own happiness is a prerequisite for being a positive influence on others. The fuller our lives become the better influence we can have on society and the significant people in our daily lives. Happy people are eager to help those in need; therefore...

Happiness is more than a selfish goal

"But isn't wanting to be happy a purely selfish pursuit?" I was asked while writing this book. It is not. As you will see, it is much more.

As we elevate our sense of well-being we instinctively want to raise other people's moods to match our own. Imagine yourself in a great mood at a family gathering while everyone else is somber. Wouldn't you rather prefer the atmosphere to be filled with love and cheer? If life on this planet can be loosely compared to a family gathering, and you are happy, wouldn't you wish everyone, including your friends, co-workers, neighbors, and everybody else with whom you interact throughout the day to share your bliss?

Luckily we can do something to improve the immediate world around us. Each of us can influence others more than we realize. And as we go about our day having a positive impact on others, their improved mood will in turn influence still more people, creating a ripple effect. We create more happiness in the world by becoming happier ourselves!

"How can a person be happy when there is so much misery in the world?" I'm frequently asked. If we take a historical viewpoint we see that ever since the beginning of life and humankind on this planet there have been natural disasters, wars, and disease. This is true now, and is likely to continue in the future (hopefully to a lesser extent). We could be happier if the world had no misery. But it does. If we choose to get depressed about all of this, we merely add to the misery. If we want to make the world a happier place it would be helpful if we first made ourselves happier. Happy people are less self-centered. They spread more positive ripples than those who are gloomy.

Increasing our happiness need not be achieved at the expense of other human beings, nor, to an extent, at the expense of living creatures. *Our freedom to pursue happiness does not give us license to infringe on someone else's right to a satisfying life.*

Truly fulfilled and happy individuals have a natural urge to improve the living conditions of society with the hope that more people have a good life. Some may decide to become active in humanitarian organizations or politics. Others may feel comfortable simply being good people and treating everyone they encounter in their daily life with honesty, love, and respect. Robert Louis Stevenson, (1850-1894) the British author, thought happiness was practically an obligation when he wrote, "There is no duty we so much underrate as the duty of being happy."

The brain: an owner's guide (how to train neurons)
It may sound strange, but we can also be happier by developing our neurons and neural pathways, and influencing the release of neurotransmitters.

Everything in our bodies– muscles, organs, skin, bones– is made up of tiny cells. This is also true of the brain. The cells in the brain are called *neurons.* An average brain has 100 billion neurons (fifteen times the population of the world). In addition to neurons, about 900 billion glial cells are present in the brain. These glial cells surround and nutritionally support the neurons.

Neurons communicate with each other through electrical impulses and chemicals. These chemicals are called *neurotransmitters.* A typical neuron has hundreds or thousands of connections, called *synapses,* with neighboring neurons. Neurotransmitters transmit messages across synapses.

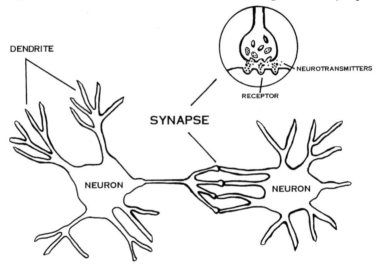

Every single external stimulation that enters through our five senses (sight, hearing, smell, touch, taste) causes tiny electrical nerve impulses and the release of minute amounts of neurotransmitters within synapses. At present, about sixty different neurotransmitters have been discovered. Some of these are *serotonin, dopamine, norepinephrine, endorphin, phenylethylamine,* and *acetylcholine.*

Every single thought or emotion (whether initiated by us or a consequence of external stimulation) is also a result of tiny electrical nerve impulses and the release of minute amounts of neurotransmitters within synapses. Reading this sentence is causing electrical nerve impulses and the release of minute amounts of neurotransmitters in certain parts of your brain. The shapes of the letters and words are being sensed by your eyes, then relayed through several pathways to your cerebral cortex. They are further interpreted in the cerebral cortex, and then converted into thoughts. These thoughts are in turn stored as memory. Memory is believed to be due to changes at synapses and the formation of protein molecules in neurons. The nature of your thoughts is dependent upon your genetic make-up, prior learning, experience, and memory. Everyone has a different brain (just like fingerprints) and no two individuals reading this paragraph will have the same exact thoughts.

Sensory input, emotions, and thoughts are associated with neurotransmitter release. The type of neurotransmitter released and the parts of the brain activated depend on what we're thinking and feeling. Warm and loving feelings toward someone stimulate a different part of the brain and release different neurotransmitters than feelings of anger or distrust.

Sensory input, emotions, and thoughts cause anatomic changes. Synapses improve and enlarge. They strengthen and become more efficient in dispatching the neurotransmitter information. *Dendrites,* the branching tree-like communicating arms of neurons where synapses are located, also enlarge. This enlargement of dendrites and synapses leads to an enhancement of neural pathways, improving communication between neurons. There are microscopic anatomical (physical) changes going on in your synapses at this moment as a result of your reading this paragraph.

Some of the neural pathways in our brain are predetermined by genetics. At birth, each infant has a different brain with unique neural connections. These neural pathways change and develop through experiences in infancy and childhood. Raising children with an abundance of love and encouragement will shape neural pathways that promote healthy self-esteem. The way parents raise children causes anatomic changes within their brain. Luckily, the brain has the ability to remodel. As adults, we still have the capacity to change and improve these neural pathways. Personal growth and self-improvement are possible.

In a fascinating experiment, two groups of mice were studied. The first group was placed in a cage and had no mental stimulation; they chaise lounged all day. The second group was trained to run through mazes. After a few weeks, half the mice who had trained were sacrificed, and their neurons were compared to the untrained group. There was a noticeable difference. The group that trained had wider and longer dendrites, more synapses, and enhanced neural pathways. The surviving half of the trained group was taken out of the stimulating environment and placed in cages. At the end of a few weeks, they were sacrificed and their brains were examined under the electron microscope. Their dendrites and synapses appeared similar to the group that had not trained. Their neurons had shrunk back.

Other studies have confirmed that when toys are placed in cages of laboratory animals, dendrites branched and synaptic connections increased noticeably in as little as four days!

The brain is similar to a muscle that grows and becomes more efficient the more it is used. The old adage, "use it or lose it," certainly applies to the brain. A tennis player develops larger neurons and improved neural pathways in the motor cortex, the part of the brain involved in musculature control. A singer or orator develops the left frontal lobe (Broca's area), the part of the brain involved with speech and language. "Practice makes perfect."

The brain is living tissue. It is far different than a computer's unmalleable hard disk. The brain grows and changes depending on its stimulation. It can become smarter, improve its capacity for memory and creativity, and generally improve in any direction in which it is stimulated. Anyone can become smarter with effort. Neural pathways that lead to bad habits can be remodeled to healthier patterns. The effect of traumatic memories can be lessened and supplanted by positive experiences. Fortunately, neurons have the capacity to change well into the last days of life. I will use the above scientific knowledge to make the following proposal:

☺ Cheerfulness, loving, positive thinking, and leading a healthy lifestyle release neurotransmitters, create changes in neurons, and develop neural pathways in ways far different from those made by repeated frowning, negative thinking, and unhealthy habits. ☹

This means that we can influence our own neurotransmitters and restructure our brain on an anatomical level by our own conscious effort, our own freewill! Since we can train our minds to be better at writing, memorizing, and creativity, we can also train to be happier! Anyone can be a 'happy athlete.' Happiness is mostly a result of healthy neural pathways and the proper amount and balance of neurotransmitters. The various happy thoughts and feelings described on page 1 may each be due to different neurotransmitters, or combinations of neurotransmitters. For instance, a joyful/fun feeling may be due to an amphetamine-type chemical such as norepinephrine. We attribute 'runner's high' to endorphins. Contented happiness may be partly due to serotonin calming certain parts of the brain. A combination of phenylethylamine and norepinephrine is likely to be involved in romance. The chemistry of happiness is still a new field; there is yet much to be learned.

These brain chemical and neural pathway changes are not to be expected overnight if bad habits and traumatic experiences have made a deep mark on the brain. Satisfying the essentials outlined in this book will lead to positive changes. This may take weeks, or in some cases, months or even years.

An additional way to influence the direction of our neural pathways is to control what enters our minds through our five senses. For instance, while watching television we can instruct our fingertips on the remote control to find an educational program rather than subject ourselves to negative and violent visual and auditory stimuli. We have the choice; to a large extent, we are our own sensory gatekeepers.

The evolutionary process has developed a brain with an intercommunicating network of over 100 billion neurons. It is truly amazing that this brain can in turn influence the secretion of its own neurotransmitters, remodel its own anatomy and influence the direction of its further development by conscious effort. Freewill, properly applied, begets more freewill. Our brain can guide itself to more happiness. (It's possible that some of these changes will be recorded in the DNA. Could 'happy genes' be passed on to progeny?)

Yes, you have freewill. You *can* be happier. Continue remodeling the most intricate, the most fascinating, the most mysterious structure in the world– the human brain. YOUR brain.

ONE

Developing a Healthy Personality

A healthy personality is the keystone to securing happiness. All traits of our personality influence happiness, especially *self-love, self-guidance,* and *attitudes.* Mental health and happiness are unlikely to be maintained if these traits are undeveloped.

Self-love is a prerequisite to warm and trusting interpersonal relationships. Similar terms that convey the concept of self-love are self-esteem, inner peace, and self-acceptance. While self-esteem is how we *think* about ourselves, self-love is how we *feel* about ourselves. Feelings can be more intense than thoughts. Self-love should not be confused with selfishness, narcissism, or vanity. When you truly love yourself you have an abundance of love to share with everyone else. The compassion and respect with which you view yourself is projected onto others.

Self-guidance is a word not found in dictionaries. I came up with it as an alternative to the word self-control. *Webster's* defines self-control as *the ability to control one's thoughts, emotions, and behavior.* I like the word 'guidance' more than 'control,' since it is gentler, less authoritarian. Therefore, I will use self-guidance to mean *the ability to guide one's thoughts, emotions, and behavior.* There are many words that are used to express this personality trait. Philosophers use the concept of *willpower.* Psychologists use the term *internal locus of control.* Some religions use the word *self-discipline.* Martial arts experts may use the word *self-mastery.*

Each of us has a different ability to self-guide depending upon our genetics, health, and environment. An individual raised in an environment of violence, inadequate parental supervision, and improper role models is likelier to be impulsive. He or she has not had the proper childhood support to develop as effective willpower as a child raised in a loving family and community.

Self-guidance influences every aspect of our personalities and lives. For instance, it enables us to postpone short-term pleasure gratification and concentrate on achieving goals. Achieving goals gives us the confidence to further improve our capacity to self-guide. By improving self-guidance, we influence the neurotransmitters released in our brains.

Toying with neurotransmitters– a note on mood-improving medicines
"Instead of putting all this effort into writing a book, why don't you just pass out prescriptions for Prozac?" quipped a friend. This is a thought-provoking question. A book on happiness needs to address the role of mood-improving medicines.

Self-guidance, or freewill, is influenced by levels of brain chemicals. We now know for certain that neurotransmitters influence personality. Anti-depressant medicines, especially the selective serotonin reuptake inhibitors (SSRIs), have given us some clues. Some of the SSRIs are Prozac (fluoxetine), Zoloft (sertraline), and Paxil (paroxetine). These medicines increase the concentration of serotonin– an important mood neurotransmitter– in the brain. Individuals with low levels of serotonin– due to genetics, environment, or both– generally display impulsive behavior. They also have a tendency for depression, aggression, alcohol abuse, and increased risk for suicide. Treatment with SSRIs has been helpful in patients with the above conditions. Patients with obsessive-compulsive disorder and those suffering with premenstrual syndrome have also been helped.

Millions of Americans have used SSRIs. Even relatively content individuals taking these medicines have noted improved self-control, enhanced mood, and better performance at work and play.

Over the next few years there will be endless discussions in the news media– pro and con– about the SSRIs and other mood-influencing medicines. The FDA is presently reviewing many new mood- or personality-improving substances for approval. Effective medicines will be manufactured to treat the shy, the impulsive, the anxious, those who want to enhance awareness, improve intelligence, and more. The urge to think, feel, or act better– even if accomplished through consuming external substances– is a natural biological drive. Alcohol is such a substance– so are nicotine and caffeine. When animals stumble across an herb, plant, or mushroom that induces pleasurable moods, they return to consume more. The urge to experience ecstasy or transcend reality through spirituality, mysticism, or consuming substances is also part of human nature. Some cultures (Native Americans, for example) have incorporated mood or awareness-enhancing substances into the rituals of their religious ceremonies.

There is no doubt that many people benefit from treatment with SSRIs, but not all do. Drawbacks to therapy with these medicines include cost and possible side effects. The cost of such therapy can exceed one thousand dollars per year. Side effects may include headache, nausea, nervousness, insomnia, and difficulty with orgasm. Psychological dependence on a pill is another factor to consider. We do not know the long-term effects of these medicines. Prozac has only been on the market since 1988. Researchers will need many more years to determine if there are any long-term health consequences. We know that there are receptors on immune cells (white blood cells for example) for neurotransmitters such as serotonin. Will taking SSRIs enhance or disturb the function of the immune system?

Mood-improving medicines can be effectively used to rouse people from their depressed lethargy just as an electric cable can be used to jump start a car's stalled battery. Thereafter, the medicines may be tapered off and replaced with other forms of therapy. If the patient relapses and other forms of therapy have not been effective, the medicines may be restarted. SSRIs affect mostly one neurotransmitter– serotonin. The approach I propose positively affects serotonin and other neurotransmitters involved in mood and personality. This complete mind-body approach has the potential to remodel our brain's neural pathways leading to a healthier adaptation to the external world. All these benefits come without side effects, unless one considers serenity and elation as side effects.

In the future, science may create medicines to prolong human lifespan. When these become available, it will be an ethical dilemma whether a person who is 'healthy and happy' can or should take substances to be 'super healthy and happy' and live longer. During the next few years each of us may have to make this personal decision. There are already substances that have prolonged lifespan in laboratory animals. Deprenyl (selegiline), a medicine presently used for Parkinson's disease, has prolonged lifespan in healthy rats when started at middle age. It is also a mood-enhancer. Melatonin, a natural pineal gland hormone that induces sleep at night, similarly has prolonged lifespan in middle-aged mice. (Melatonin is now available in health food stores.) Could the same benefits hold true in humans? It's possible, but no long-term human studies are available. It will take decades of careful studies before we find definite answers. For instance, after so many years of studying the effects of estrogen replacement therapy in postmenopausal women, we still don't know for certain whether the benefits significantly outweigh the risks.

I believe that in order for us to be happier and become our best, all knowledge and means available should be used. If laboratory-synthesized substances are shown by science to improve the quality of our lives and life expectancy, why not take advantage of them? After all, throughout history, humankind has used intelligence to continually improve health and well-being. Immunizations against various illnesses have enormously influenced longevity, adding many years to life expectancy. Vitamin supplements have also come to us via science. Antioxidants such as vitamins C and E are thought to prolong lifespan. A study done at the University of California at Los Angeles followed over 11,000 people for a number of years. Those who had taken vitamin C supplements (at least 250 mg) lived one to two years longer. It is possible to ingest that much vitamin C through consistently eating many fresh fruits and vegetables a day. However, one cannot ingest enough vitamin E through foods for maximal beneficial effects. Studies show that taking over 100 units of vitamin E a day reduces the risk for heart disease and cancer. Even a good diet barely supplies a fraction (20 to 30 units) of what may be optimal (100 to 600 units). A complete approach to happiness would therefore include anything and everything that works, whether natural or laboratory-fashioned.

It is too early to predict the long-term health consequences– beneficial or damaging– of the use of mood-improving medicines. If after fulfilling the essentials discussed in this book you still have a low mood, have an open discussion with your physician. If both of you agree to give SSRIs, deprenyl, or other mood-enhancers a try, use the lowest effective dose– perhaps half or a quarter of the regular dose. In a future printing– as more scientific knowledge becomes available– I hope to make a more definitive recommendation about the use of these new pharmaceutical agents. A fuller discussion of these medicines is provided in the appendix.

The modern world is evolving at dizzying speeds. For better or for worse we're no longer living through the tortoise-pace changes of previous ages. Our society requires that we quickly adapt. One aspect of developing a healthy personality is through flexibility– remaining open to new possibilities (in all areas of life) and accepting the recommendations of science. By doing so we become healthier and happier, and live longer. Science is not always right, but it has the ability to correct itself as new information becomes available.

Through my many years of practice as a family physician I have learned the importance of considering the whole person in any type of healing or self-improvement. The following are some approaches that lead to self-improvement: *cognitive* (developing a healthy personality), *humanistic* (learning empathy and warmth, cultivating a sense of connection), *introspective* (healing emotional wounds, psychotherapy, catharsis), *behavioral* (pursuing meaningful goals, finding satisfying work, pleasure gratification), *practical* (having financial security, a comfortable place to live), and *biological* (diet, vitamins, herbs, nutrients, medicines).

On the path to a healthier personality

The beginning of wisdom is the realization that we can improve our ability to self-guide and develop more positive attitudes.

"A mind…" wrote John Milton (1608-74), the English poet, "Can make a heaven of hell, a hell of heaven." I'd like to share with you an experience that influenced me. It happened– as the nursery rhyme goes– "One misty, moisty morning, when cloudy was the weather…"

On one of my bicycle trips through Europe, I was riding at dawn through the isolated, misty moors of Dorset, England (the setting for Thomas Hardy's novel *Tess of the D'Urbervilles*). Low clouds fogged into the hills as I climbed the narrow winding path past curiously gazing sheep.

I had been riding for two weeks having started from London, staying overnight at quaint village inns. Thus far, the weather had been surprisingly accommodating. This particular October morning, however, the mist was casually followed by a drizzle and then a downpour. There was no cover. I was miles away from any village. As the rain intensified, the drops soaked their way through my clothing. Shallow mudpools formed on the path as the rolling bicycle wheels streamed brown droplets over my legs, socks, and shoes. My morning ride was rapidly shifting into an unpleasant course.

Suddenly, I chose to change my response. I tried a smile. Looking up towards the clouds I felt the sensation of raindrops splashing on my face. I opened my mouth and allowed the water drops to land on my tongue. Instead of resisting my circumstance, I accepted it. Another facet of nature's wondrous variety was being manifested.

I dismounted and walked the bike. A renewed vigor coursed through my veins. The rains had brought a freshness to the morning and all was still except for the intermittent echoes of bleating sheep. A magical beauty enveloped the hills as the fragrance of the moist heather breezed by my nostrils. The thirsty, emerald-colored moss layering the centuries-old stone hedges revived from its arid slumber. A sense of wonder prevailed amid this fog-bound heath.

By midday, the clouds, drained of their reserves, partially parted, splaying the sun into a multitude of rainbow-hued rays. Eventually the clouds separated, revealing the sun in its full splendor. The warm rays dried my rain-showered clothes. I had never appreciated the sun more than I did that day. The entire morning turned out to be not only exhilarating, but an attitude-molding milestone.

We have more guidance on our thoughts and behavior than we realize. The manner of our response to an external factor is often more important than the inherent goodness or badness of the factor itself. *Ultimately, it is our response that determines the meaning to anything that happens to us.*

My former roommate Christine was yelled at by her boyfriend while they were discussing their plans for the evening. She had the option to yell back magnifying the dispute but chose to calmly open the lines of communication and understand the motivation behind the outburst. He claimed he was always the one who was flexible and willing to compromise. They openly discussed this and resolved his anger. Christine admitted he had a point. They developed a deeper bonding.

Evelyn, a mother of three active children, wanted some relaxing pills. "My kids are driving me crazy." I discussed with her what her expectations and attitudes were about child rearing. She told me about her mother who frequently yelled at her while she was growing up. Her mother was always frantic; nothing around the house seemed under control. Evelyn grew up thinking that that's how family life is. After three weekly discussions with her about healthier ways to run a household, she realized that most of the tension in her house was fueled by her overreaction to minor episodes. She was able to change her behavior and become calmer without medicines. Interestingly, her children also became calmer.

Tom, a physician colleague, had a tendency to have one too many beers at parties. One evening he slammed into a car. The car was totaled; luckily the driver was not hurt. His insurance rates skyrocketed. Tom, however, did not get upset at the rise. Instead, he chose to make the best of the situation. He considered the accident a warning and has since not driven his car under the influence.

In my twenties I remember being restless while waiting in line at the checkout counter at the grocery store. Now I leaf through periodicals or strike up a conversation with people in line. I've picked up many tidbits of information from magazines I wouldn't normally buy and read. Waiting in line no longer annoys me.

Each circumstance is an opportunity to grow and learn, in a calm and serene manner. There is no need to react with tension or anger. We can choose the way we respond to situations. Studies show that daily hassles impinge more upon physical and mental health than infrequent tragic events. Our immune system promptly responds to our moods. Stress interferes with the function of white blood cells, making us more susceptible to colds and other infections. Transcend the annoyance of these mundane occurrences by guiding your thoughts and actions toward better options. "Experience is not what happens to you," Aldous Huxley (1894-1963), the English writer, counseled, "it is what you do with what happens."

Whenever confronted with a situation that appears unfortunate or unpleasant, follow this process of inquiry:

- Why did it happen? Could I have prevented it?
- Since it has happened, can I learn something from it? As a result of this experience, can I grow in wisdom?
- Is it possible to turn this around to an eventual advantage by using my intelligence, creativity, and perseverance?

"By happy alchemy of mind, they turn to pleasure all they find," penned Matthew Green (1696-1737), the English poet. Each situation may be viewed as either a stumbling block or stepping stone. If you have little self-guidance at this point in your life, don't despair– you can develop this personality trait. With time, we continue profiting from our life experiences. We have little self-guidance when young. If a toy is taken away from a three year old, the child may start crying. Teenagers have more self-control than children, yet have variable mood swings: a pimple can create havoc in a teenager's emotional state; rejection from a heart-throb can wound deeply. As adults, we are less affected by external circumstances. When something unpleasant happens, we realize it's not the end of the world. We can deal with the problem. Each of us will develop varying skills in achieving inner guidance and coping with the outside world. It is something we can continuously work on and improve. With time, we can all grow into majestic trees, secured by deep roots, little affected by the winds and storms of misfortune. Next time you are asked, "How's life treating you?" answer confidently, "I'm treating it well."

It is extremely unlikely that everything will go our way in life. Eventually, we all encounter situations that are contrary to our hopes and desires. A great deal of unhappiness and disappointment may follow unrealistic expectations that life will unfold with our best interest in mind. Life owes us nothing. This planet evolves indifferently to humankind's happiness. Hurricanes course indiscriminately— sweeping along the 'good,' the 'bad,' and everyone in between. Earthquakes shudder the ground above, unconcerned with the welfare of buildings, highways, and people. Once we accept the reality that life provides us no guarantees and no obligations, we stop lamenting "why me?" Instead, we learn to grow from each experience, optimistically trying to make the best of each situation. We start developing healthier beliefs and *attitudes,* beginning a process of reappreciation. Everything we already have may be viewed as life's gift. We become ever grateful for our health, our loved ones, that we have enough food, clothing, shelter and the infinite blessings we take for granted. We are happiest when we expect nothing— and appreciate *everything.*

It hurts to give up wishful thinking— that we are immune from misfortune and tragedy, that life is looking out for us, that we have special protection and privileges. In the short run, accepting reality makes some people unhappy. In the long run, and for most people, accepting reality helps us adapt to the world more easily and leads to more consistent long-term happiness.

Attitudes are defined as *predispositions to think and respond consistently to some person, object, or situation.* One way to develop healthier attitudes is by...

Learning the art of reappreciation
Fostering a healthy attitude can result in immediate psychological changes. If we reappreciate everything we already have, then there are many reasons to be happy. If we choose not to be content with our present situa-

tion in life (unless it happens to be extraordinarily difficult), the future will probably not provide happiness either.

Humans easily adapt to new circumstances. As a child, do you remember the pleasure a birthday toy initially provided... and how quickly this pleasure vanished? As a teenager, wasn't it exciting the first time you drove a car? Now, sitting behind the wheel has likely lost the appeal it had in the early days. Similarly, almost any new state that is achieved in life, whether it be wealth, romance, or fame, slowly loses its allure. Initially, a new situation feels marvelous. After an interval, the novelty fades. Take money as an example. Lottery winners are euphoric upon discovering they hold the winning ticket. This euphoria is not permanent. After a few months, many of the winners are not significantly happier than before. In the long run, a rise in income every year may induce more happiness than a sudden lottery jackpot win.

When I first began to work as a cruise ship physician I thrived on the attention showered on me. I wore a well-tailored white suit with three-striped epaulets. Ship passengers approached me to start conversations, often buying me drinks. Being the doctor on the cruise ship was akin to being a celebrity on land. Even though I enjoyed the attention, there were times when I just wanted to go up on deck and be by myself; leaning against the banister to watch the distant horizon, lost in my own solitude... the salty sea breeze caressing my cheeks, playing with my hair. But, invariably, I would be approached by a passenger who would ask the questions I had grown accustomed to: "What's it like to work as a cruise ship doctor?" "Is this ship anything like the *Love Boat*?" "What's the worst medical emergency you've ever had?"

I was always polite and cheerful in answering these questions, as if it was the first time I had ever heard them asked. I learned from this experience. Being the center of attention can have its drawbacks. Later, I moved to Marina Del Rey, California. It was so exciting to take a walk on the beach each evening after a long day at the office. Within a few months the walks had lost their original excitement.

Our senses adapt to new situations and require *absence, variety, ever increasing stimulation, or change in attitude* for reappreciation.

Since each new situation in our lives eventually loses some, if not all, of its appeal, we need to take a moment to reflect on our present circumstances in order to see them with a new attitude. Marcel Proust (1871-1922), the French novelist, remarked, "The real voyage of discovery consists not in seeking new lands, but in seeing with new eyes." A change in attitude allows a reappreciation of everything we already have. It is a wonderful feeling to go through this process, as if meeting and hugging old friends.

Have you ever lost a purse, wallet, or other important possession and after a period of time recovered it? Do you remember what a relief it was? How good it felt? If we nurture this same approach in life, being thankful that everything we already have is a gift or blessing, we find instant reasons to be happier. Let's learn to reappreciate the following:

Health

Until an accident or illness occurs, we do not usually think about our health. Why wait until jolted by a traumatic event or debilitating condition to value it? Having worked in hospitals and emergency rooms, I have seen, first-hand, accidents and other tragedies that can befall people.

I have heard countless pleas from patients. George, a forty-six year old optometrist with kidney stones moaned, "Doctor, if I could only urinate without pain, I'd be the happiest person on earth." Sandra, a thirty-six year old financial analyst noting a lump in her breast averred, "If the biopsy shows this lump is not a cancer, I'll never complain again about anything my entire life." Bill, a sixty-six year old engineer, was suffering from esophageal cancer. After a stomach tube was placed through his abdomen for feedings, he hopelessly said, "I never thought I would lose the ability to taste food and swallow while alive." Ann, a twenty-three year old aspiring actress, was injured in a motorcycle accident losing most of her upper teeth. She cried, "It's so hard to eat an apple with false teeth. I wish so much I could turn back time."

Suffering has certain advantages: it lowers our expectation level. Simple things in life, such as urinating painlessly, biting into an apple, and tasting food, seem precious. If the suffering is the result of a reversible condition, such as a kidney stone that passes returning the urinary system to normal flow, the experience may be beneficial– if we learn from it. Suffering also reminds us to have empathy for those who are, likewise, going through difficult times. However, we need not wait until hardship makes a personal, unwelcome visit in order to be grateful *every day* that we are healthy.

Important people in our lives

It often takes a calamity such as death, cancer, or a serious accident before we realize how important loved ones are. Treat everyone who is important to you as if they only had a short time to live, be it your spouse, mother, father, child, sibling or friend. As a result of this change in attitude, you may find yourself getting involved in fewer disputes while developing deeper bonds.

Possessions

Happiness does not necessarily depend on how much we own, rather, it depends on our attitude: *how well we enjoy what we already possess.* The content owner of a few pairs of shoes is 'richer' than the insatiable possessor of roomfuls. Do you remember Imelda Marcos with her collection of over 1,000 pairs? Resist the tendency to compare what you have with that of your friends, neighbors, and celebrities.

There will always be someone who is wealthier, owns a nicer house, drives a more expensive car, is more attractive, or has a more beautiful spouse or lover. If you find yourself in this *I wish for what others have* predicament, don't despair; it need not be so. As you become happier by improving your attitude, connecting with others on an intimate level, finding a passionate purpose in life, and satisfying some of the other essentials discussed in this book, you'll drift into your own blissful island of *live and let live* self-content. The thought of coveting the possession of others will not even cross your mind.

Further along the appreciation path

If you are reading this book it is fair to assume that you have a roof over your head and adequate sustenance and clothing; your essential needs for survival have been met.

There is so much for which we need to be grateful. We live in a politically stable country with a high standard of living, providing us with the basic framework necessary for the pursuit of happiness. Sometimes we forget that the majority of people living in this world survive under harsh political conditions with few modern comforts. (Unfortunately, even in our own wealthy country, there are unacceptable numbers of disadvantaged people.) Let's take a moment to reflect on what we often take for granted.

We are sheltered from the extremes of nature in our secure dwellings. Energy is plentiful. Our homes are well heated in the coldest winter months and cooled during oppressive heat waves. Indoor plumbing, hot water, and all modern conveniences are readily tapped. Water is accessible in unlimited quantities. Food is plentiful. Even kings and emperors of the past could not indulge in all the fruits and vegetables that are readily available to us during all seasons. The thought of starving does not cross our minds. Do you say your thanks before a meal? We rarely, if ever, stop, contemplate, and feel grateful at the cornucopia of goods overflowing in stores and shopping malls.

Progress in medicine has prolonged life expectancy and reduced misery from illness. The average life expectancy has risen from about fifty (in 1900) to over seventy (in the 1990's)– with the scientific promise of even greater lifespan extension. Pain medicines and anesthesia have taken away much physical suffering. Until the last century, patients underwent surgery and amputations with little or no pain relief. Mothers and fathers lost their tender children from preventable or curable illnesses such as polio, meningitis, and diarrhea. Eyeglasses and contact lenses correct our vision to see the world in its full splendor. Can you imagine going through life seeing everything blurred as people in previous centuries did? As many of the poor in third world countries still do?

Welfare and unemployment benefits provide a safety net for those experiencing difficult financial times. In case of emergency, ambulances, police, and fire departments respond promptly. Advances in transportation allow us to travel practically anywhere on this planet, and possibly beyond. We have one of the best National Park systems in the world, providing us with a vast wilderness for exploration and solitude. The list of our blessings is quite long.

Take a moment now or later and list some of the blessings that you normally take for granted. Write down at least one from each category: health, loved ones, possessions, and miscellaneous. Make a private list of everything you cherish and periodically say to yourself "I'm glad I have... (fill in the blank)."

Periodically sit alone and imagine everything that is important to you. Reflect on your health, parents, siblings, friends, home, car, clothes, spouse or lover, or anything else you cherish. Now imagine all of these blessings gone. Picture how difficult and horrible this would be. In your mind, one by one, introduce each item or person back into your life. Can you believe how happy you would be if you lost everything you now have... and after a period of time they all returned?

Every moment of our existence is precious. It is futile to postpone happiness until everything is right and all the problems on this planet are solved. Perfect personal and planetary harmony may never be. When will you start being happier? Not next year. Not next month. Not next week. Not even tomorrow or later today.

Be happier starting now!

The initial step towards being happier can begin simply by accessing your freewill. Create more happiness! A simple upward curving of the corners of the mouth is a good start. The way we behave influences our thoughts and emotions. Studies show that it works! By flexing a few smile muscles we elevate our mood. There is a neural feedback which goes from our facial muscles back to our brain. Psychologists call it the 'facial feedback hypothesis.' EEGs (electroencephalograms) show that different parts of the brain are activated in subjects who smile than in those who frown. Positive moods stimulate the left frontal side of the brain while negative moods stimulate the right frontal side. Furthermore, deliberate smiles generate some of the same physiological changes as spontaneous smiles during times of good mood. Researchers find that those who behave happily are more likely to become happy. I hypothesize that the contraction of 'smile' facial muscles triggers the release of mood-elevating neurotransmitters. It's as simple as this: *Pretend you are happier and you will be genuinely happier.*

Have you ever been in a downcast mood but had to attend a social gathering? After forcing a merry disposition and pretending you were in a good mood, do you remember the improved sense of well being that often followed?

Wake up each morning, smile, and decide to have a pleasant day. Consciously remind yourself to smile frequently throughout the day whether you are alone or around others. As you go about your routine, your happy expression will be contagious. Your cheerful disposition will influence the mood of those whose lives you touch on a daily basis.

Place ☺ stickers on your mirrors, bedroom walls, telephones, and anywhere else you wish to remind yourself throughout the day. An especially important place for a smile sticker is on the inner-side of your home's front door. This sticker will remind you to be in a good mood before leaving for work or school in the morning. All these stickers may appear silly or childish, but it is through repetition that we remodel our brain to be happier. Just like learning how to play the piano or acquiring any skill, mood elevation takes practice. After a few weeks of this practice you don't have to continue smiling as often. Your brain has remodeled its neural pathways and a few smile reminders throughout the day are enough to keep you in a good mood. If you reduce your smile frequency and notice yourself not as happy, return to frequent smiling.

Participants in a psychology experiment were asked to flash various facial expressions at strangers in public places. Smiles were greeted with a return smile half the time, while frowns were rarely returned. Another study found that those flashing a smile were perceived to be more honest and trustworthy. Furthermore, job applicants who smiled were more likely to be hired than nonsmilers. Smiling waiters received bigger tips. Police officers were more likely to give warnings than tickets to drivers who were cheerful.

A happy person makes friends more easily. It is human nature that we want to be around others who have an upbeat mood– and who make us feel better.

Smiling, improved self-guidance, and positive attitudes point to the proper path. There is more to explore. I invite you to join me on a spiritual journey– a journey of heart-happiness.

TWO

Cultivating a Sense of Connection

One word
frees us from all
the weight and pain of life.
That word is Love.
Sophocles (495-406 BCE)

The urge to connect is a fundamental drive in every culture throughout all lands and regions of our globe, from the African Bushmen roaming the baked Kalahari desert to Alaskan Eskimos bivouacked in igloos. Historical and archeological evidence suggests that this urge has been present as far back as recorded time, and for good reason. People who develop the ability to connect lead healthier and happier lives.

The need for connection may be fulfilled several ways. On a personal level we connect with fellow human beings through friendship, physical intimacy, romance, marriage, and family. Personal connection is also accomplished with cats, dogs, and other animals. We satisfy the urge to belong to something larger than ourselves by joining religious, humanistic, or philosophic groups. We dedicate our efforts to political, environmental, and charitable causes, and identify with companies, universities, sports teams, ethnic groups, communities, and nations. Partly due to our fear of mortality, we strive to connect and attach to a spiritual power greater and more permanent than ourselves. Many attempt this relationship with *God*. New Agers and followers of some Eastern religions identify with a *Universal Consciousness* or *Life Force*. Others may feel comfortable connecting simply with nature's *here and now*. The foundation of happiness solidifies as we branch wider, touch, connect, and continue a lifelong journey of growth.

Prehistoric men and women bonded on an intimate level by belonging to a tribe. On a larger scale, they connected with nature and the cosmos through spirits perceived in fauna, flora, prominent geological features, the moon and sun. Some tribes also worshiped *God(s)* or *Big Spirit(s)*.

In modern times it has become increasingly difficult to develop a true sense of connection with one another and *Mother Earth*. Many of us, or our loved ones, have moved to regions distant from where we grew up. The sense of community, so important in providing a feeling of being grounded, has weakened. The growing impersonality of the megalopolis; megalithic, steel skyscrapers; concrete, multi-level superhighways; characterless suburban developments with endless extensions; isolated, boxed, *Andy Warhol Campbell Soup*-like apartment buildings; neighbors who are strangers; crowds and crowds of nameless faces; families split apart through discord; friends and acquaintances who frequently relocate; and television, video, and movie addiction that has transformed us into self-absorbed spectators have all made long-term intimate bonding a challenge.

Even in these modern, infertile grounds, it is possible to sow the seeds of intimacy. By cultivating more meaningful relationships, we reap the harvest of love and happiness.

In order to culture mature human relationships, we first need to connect with ourselves– to love ourselves. Self-love is the underlying prerequisite for mental health. As discussed in chapter one, self-love and self-esteem are closely related but differ in the following respect: self-esteem is how we *think* about ourselves while self-love is how we *feel* about ourselves. Feelings are more intense than thoughts.

Love yourself because
you are you,
unique.
There is no one else
exactly like you.

32

Love yourself because
you hurt
you feel
you care
you cry
you are human.
You deserve to be loved–
especially by you.

Self-love

Genuine love begins deep inside us. By loving and accepting ourselves, a sense of peace and harmony silently spreads all through us, muting any notes of discord. Alone no longer means lonely. Time spent alone is cherished, not feared. Our restless search for serenity at faraway shores and through outside sources ends. We finally return back to ourselves. At last we understand that *home* is wherever we are. *At all times, we are home.*

The journey towards self-love has infinite rewards. An adventure in growth and self-discovery, gratifying at every step, self-love provides greater satisfaction than fine garments, gold, or a coffer of gems.

Self-love is not based on physical appearance. It should make little difference whether we are lanky, fat, short, disabled, pimpled, elderly, or have honeydew- or lime-sized breasts. Love, by its very nature, transcends. No matter what we look like, we are all a marvel of creation. Friedrich Nietzsche, the German philosopher, echoed a similar thought: "At bottom every *(wo)*man knows well enough that *(s)*he is a unique being, only once on this earth; and by no extraordinary chance will such a marvelously picturesque piece of diversity in unity... ever be put together a second time."

Loving ourselves is a decision– *our decision*. It is not based on our past, nor is it based on what other people think or feel about us.

Unconditional self-love can begin at any moment. Take a few minutes and write down a few reasons why you should love yourself. These may include your natural talents, virtuous qualities, and *imperfections*. Include character flaws and shortcomings that you have accepted within yourself, but are trying to improve. Self-love doesn't mean that we shouldn't continue to change and become better. However, it liberates us from desperately seeking approval through outside eyes.

Oscar Wilde, the Irish writer, affirmed, "To love oneself is the beginning of a life-long romance." I began to love myself in my early twenties. It has made all the difference in being a happy person.

I love *me*.
I love me *the way I am*.
I love me the way I am *right now*.

Write this affirmation on your bedroom mirror and above your bed. Reminders and repetitions are more helpful than we realize. Make this affirmation a continuing, ongoing part of your life.

Self-love is more than a selfish goal since it secures a personal foundation from which universal love can expand. The more we accept ourselves and our imperfections, the less we judge or criticize others. The gentleness and compassion with which we view ourselves naturally projects on those we encounter in our daily lives. We cannot be at peace with anyone until the dove of peace is securely nested within us.

Once we begin the process of self-love, we naturally wish to share our love with those around us. Extending beyond ourselves is done willingly. This sharing springs forth from inner abundance, not obligation.

My love for me grows
and grows each day more
filling my fountain core.
Reaching the rim, overflows...
gently flows beyond my wall
and spreads... spreads to embrace all.

As our inner fountain begins to fill, a gratifying realization dawns. We now have more self-confidence. Since we are less emotionally dependent on others, we radiate love and warmth as does the sun. Our rays touch near and far to brighten people's lives, expecting nothing in return. Healthy love does not expect reciprocation; it pours out from an inner abundance. A wonderful consequence of this outpouring– this radiation–

is the love reflected back to us, providing additional warmth to our daily lives. The more we love, the more lovable we become. The more we accept others, the more they will accept us, give us positive feedback, and further nourish our self-love. If we want to be loved, we need to love first.

If the love we feel and express is not returned, we cannot lose. The real satisfaction of love is in the loving– feeling it within ourselves. What benefit is it to us if we are showered by adulation (for instance, being famous or extremely good-looking), but have not developed the capacity to feel love within?

Universal Love

> "Love is patient; love is kind; love is not envious or boastful or arrogant or rude. It does not insist on its own way; it is not irritable or resentful; it does not rejoice in wrongdoing, but rejoices in the truth. It bears all things, believes all things, hopes all things, endures all things. Love never ends..."
> The Bible, *First Epistle to the Corinthians*, 13:4-8

Universal love is a natural extension of our self-love. It is also a learned art. Every moment of every day we benefit by reminding ourselves to put aside our anger, jealousy, judgmental attitude, and grudges. By urging ourselves to feel warmth and fondness for everyone, no matter how different they are (race, beliefs, age, gender, or sexual orientation), our outlook changes. We learn how to empathize, to see things from another's point of view. Rather than focusing on people's shortcomings, we focus on their positive attributes. Instead of looking for differences between *us* and *them*, we find common bonds that we share. Each and every person has exquisite qualities. We see the heart of an innocent, sensitive child within each person. All of us are children deep inside.

Universal love has no limits. As we allow ourselves to grow, we connect more deeply with people and our natural surroundings. Everything and everybody appear beautiful and perfect– just the way they are. In our daily lives, we begin to reappreciate and embrace our family, friends, neighbors, and co-workers. We expand our love to include the poor, sick, disabled, and those less fortunate than ourselves. We even appreciate things we previously considered unpleasant or unattractive.

Expansion may involve our love for animals. We can feel fondness for our pet cat curled on the sofa and for a solitary, northern wolf crossing windswept, frozen tundra. The more we expand, the more there is to appreciate. We can grow to appreciate all aspects of this wondrous planet. The infinite patterns of sand on the beach, the marvels of human architectural creations, a fragile flower petal waving in the breeze, a meandering brook flowing quietly through an evergreen forest, are all there for us to connect with and cherish. The more we view the outside world as continuous with our inner beauty, the more we feel at home on this earth.

Love can be expanded or contracted: it is our choice. The only restrictions are those we self-impose. With time, we can discover more possibilities for growth.

A modest exercise in expansion

Universal love is more easily nurtured in a state of relaxation. Find a comfortable, quiet place to sit or lie down. Take a slow, deep breath, and slowly exhale through your nostrils. Repeat this process a few more times. Do you feel stress anywhere? Relax your shoulders and any other body parts that may be tense. Close your eyes and take a few more deep breaths.

Now let your thoughts float freely... there is no need to resist anything that comes to your mind... you will find that you can choose to interpret wandering thoughts– of people, animals, plants, things, events– in any way you wish. In this quiet, safe place, accept these thoughts with warmth and affection without judgment or blame. See and feel the beauty around you. It is always there.

There is no need to wait for that *one and only* special person to unlock your chest and free the love within you. Expanding your love is within your immediate control. In your daily life, you can expand anytime, anywhere. Don't be discouraged if you don't feel anything right away. With persistence, moment after moment, day after day, you will begin to experience it. As with learning a new language or art, loving becomes easier once the initial inertia is overcome. Thereafter, it grows on itself as long as you look for the positive aspects of people and events.

"Let those love now who never loved before," urged Thomas Parnell (1679-1718), the British writer. He continued, "Let those who always loved, now love the more." We *can* love more. Leading a complete and balanced lifestyle allows positive feelings to bud and blossom. It's harder to reap the harvest of love if we are stressed, weakened by poor health, worried about finances, or burdened by other grave matters.

Viewing everything with universal love influences our dreams. They become friendlier. The interpersonal encounters that I recall in my dreams have become much more nurturing since adopting an open heart and letting go of grudges. A few years ago, I had a dispute with a friend. We stopped speaking to each other and lost contact. Recently, I had a dream that I was hugging him.

During the course of writing this book it dawned on me that I should combine feelings of joy with the affection and warmth that results from viewing the world with an open heart. This merging of feelings is a synergistic delight. Savor this remarkable combination each and every moment. Lead the rest of your life bathed in this blissful state. Ripple happy hearts far and wide.

If you can't initially blend both emotions, start with a smile for a while. Then practice opening your heart. When you are comfortable with both, combine them.

The more you expand, the richer life will be for you and those whose lives you touch. The world becomes as meaningful as your expansion. By feeling self- and universal love, some of you will notice that you are beginning to live on a higher level of consciousness.

The art of self-transcendence

By flowing beyond our fountain wall, we blur the boundaries between self and environment. We become more compassionate, caring, and sensitive to the welfare of humanity. A deeper concern evolves for the health of our planet as we consider it an extension of ourselves. This concept of 'expansion' is emphasized in some religions or beliefs where the thinning of the ego boundary– leading to union with the oneness or infiniteness of the universe– is the ultimate goal.

A deep sense of self-love and dissolved ego boundaries allow a *perception* that our minds have levitated above our bodies. We witness ourselves going through the drama of daily life from an external perspective. Through this higher state of consciousness, we gain further insight. We transcend the aggravations of daily existence, side-step quarrels and arguments. We find no reason to get angry to the point of disputes. No one can say anything to hurt our dissolved egos. We stop taking ourselves too seriously. When on the receiving end of a joke or prank, we laugh along heartily. If yelled at, we respond calmly.

We lose our obsession to win at the expense of someone else. Since we are satisfied with ourselves and have enough, we begin to enjoy the game of life and are glad when fortune visits others. Self-contentment and a proper attitude enable us to derive pleasure from the success and accomplishment of others. Follow Berton Braley (1882-1950), the American writer's generous advice, "And if I should lose, let me stand by the road and cheer as the winner goes by."

Self-love and universal love can be incorporated in our daily lives on a practical level.

Relationships and friendships
When our own lives glow with inner fullness and abundance, people naturally gravitate toward us. Happy and loving people are magnets.

Everyone is trying to survive in this world as best they know how. It is amazing how good it feels when we approach every interaction with compassion and love instead of constant analysis and judgement. The more we judge and criticize the behavior of others, the more we limit our own happiness.

Just like a boomerang, the energy we radiate often returns to us. If we are loving, we encounter kindness and warmth. If we act mean and rude, we can only expect to be treated the same. Quid pro quo. The choice is ours. Mo Ti (450 BCE), the Chinese philosopher, taught "Those who love others will be loved in return. Do good to others and others will do good to you. Hate people and be hated by them. Hurt them and they will hurt you. What is hard about that?"

The art of friendship

In the company of a true friend, we feel comfortable. Periods of total silence are passed at ease. A sense of sharing, trust, and mutual care permeates. We know that we can pour out our hearts, both the chaff and grain, and still be accepted. A kind ear listens to our worries and concerns. A kind voice soothes with compassionate words. The love and connection between friends is immensely rewarding. True friends are there for us during times of sorrow and hardship. We can rely on them as they can rely on us when misfortune visits. Real friends celebrate with us during times of good fortune. They share our excitement when we are successful, without feeling threatened or jealous.

Because we are influenced by the people around us, it is best to choose as our closest friends those who share a path of self-growth. Good friends have the inner abundance to encourage and nourish us. They water our roots on our way to becoming a beautiful, blooming tree. We, in turn, encourage them to develop their full potential.

Every person we encounter has the potential to be a friend forever. The possibilities of new friendships are plentiful. Without preconceived limitations, we welcome people who may be different than us. We focus on common bonds and appreciate the fascinating rainbow-tinted tapestry characterizing each human. There is inner beauty in everyone. Why focus on imperfections? Why focus on differences? The more we accept others, the more we are accepted by them.

Having many friends is important, though the quality of friendships is more meaningful than quantity.

Strive to be on good terms with everybody whether the relationship is private or business. Holding grudges and contemplating revenge squander energy. Alienating people and having enemies is unwise. We are successful in our private lives and career not only by *what* we know, but *who* we know, and how well we get along with everybody.

The art of communication

Verbal interaction is a crucial part of friendships and relationships. While involved in any type of interaction, remember that thoughts are not telepathic. If something concerns us, it needs to be verbalized. Expecting our friend, lover, spouse, or other people to read our mind is unreasonable. Express concerns in a non-threatening manner; avoid placing the other person in a defensive position.

Like all art forms, conversation is best done in a relaxed manner. Take full deep breaths by expanding the belly. There is no reason to be tense. Enjoy the company of others by accepting them the way they are regardless of status, age, race, sex or attractiveness. Think warm and loving feelings. The positive energy you radiate will return to you.

Listening is an inherent part of communication. A good listener makes a strong attempt to understand each person's thoughts and feelings. The ability to see things from another's point of view is crucial to the art of communication.

Different childhood and adult experiences shape and mold each one of us. We learn from every encounter if we understand and respect individual uniqueness. It is enjoyable to debate and exchange ideas, but this need not lead to arguments. At the least, we may wish to acknowledge the grain of truth in whatever someone says. *There are as many points of view as there are people on this planet.* During a discussion a better option to saying, "You are wrong," would be, "I have a different perspective on this issue," or, "I respect your point of view and would like to share mine with you." When people feel understood, they are more receptive to our point of view.

Self-confidence allows us to acknowledge mistakes. If we hurt anyone thru words or deeds, apologies are appropriate. It's never too soon, never too late to say, "I'm sorry." People admire our courage when we say, "I made a mistake."

There's something pleasing about hearing one's own name. At parties or business meetings, call people by name at least once during a conversation. This creates an instant connection.

Be the first to say "hello." It is amazing how much we learn by conversing with varied individuals. The course of your life can be changed by a chance encounter with one person!

The manner in which "hello" is said when answering a phone call or meeting someone sets the tone for the conversation. A cheerful greeting and smile reciprocate a similar response.

The arts of criticism and praise (speak softly and carry a big plume)
Words can wound as painfully as swords. We have so much power at the tip of our tongues. Why not use gentle words to encourage and support, instead of hurting others?

As we develop self-love, it becomes easier to be generous with praise and compliments since we want to elevate people's mood to match our own. Say a kind word to someone daily and lift their spirits. A few kind words, sincerely spoken, do wonders to the giver and receiver. Positive words return to us, as does love.

When we speak in a positive manner, we feel better. Complaining and criticizing intensify discontent. What we say influences how we feel and what we think.

Although best avoided, criticism is more effective when started with a compliment and then said as gently as possible, making an effort not to hurt feelings. End the conversation with another compliment– the 'Sandwich style' or 'Oreo approach.' Criticizing in public stirs up anger; it's properly done behind closed doors. A Russian proverb aptly summarizes, "I praise loudly, I blame softly." When we least expect it, a criticism spoken behind someone's back may be discovered.

A mother, with her little daughter, was visiting a neighbor. The girl suddenly said, "Mrs. Miller, may I see your new kitchen tiles?" "Certainly, Colleen. How kind of you to be interested!" The girl went into the kitchen and soon reappeared. "Gee, mommy," she said puzzled, "It didn't make *me* sick."

Those who frequently criticize are often unhappy with themselves and have low self-esteem. Their criticisms may be projections of their inability to accept their own imperfections. They may have kind hearts hidden under layers of prickly artichoke leaves. Let's keep this in mind and see if we can help them improve their self-esteem.

Physical intimacy

Caress, feel the warmth of someone's skin, comfort and kindle the hearth within. Hug or touch others if it feels right to do so. Respect physical boundaries; not all are comfortable with their bodies or accustomed to hugs. Hugging is best done leisurely; feel the radiance without the hurry to let go of the embrace. A friendly touch helps us connect.

Touching has an enormous impact on people. In a study done to determine the effect of touch on human behavior, a researcher purposely left coins in a phone booth. Individuals entering the booth noticed the coins and would pocket them. As each caller came out of the booth, the researcher tried two approaches. Those who were plainly asked if they had found any coins said "no" in most cases. Those who were lightly touched on the forearm while being asked if they had found any coins were more likely to admit the truth.

What about sexual intimacy? Almost every human being with a healthy physiology has a libido. This is an incredibly powerful drive, especially in teenagers and young adults as the glands relentlessly pump and pump like the incessant tempo of a high school marching band. But where do we go with a libido? Our culture provides us with mixed messages about sexual intimacy. Some voices equate fulfilling the urge for sexual bonding as a failure in self-control. Others promote sex as the most satisfying aspect of life. The result is confusion– a conflict between the internal forces of natural desire and those of externally induced guilt.

Physical intimacy *can* be a delight without genital contact. Oftentimes, the most wonderful and cherished experiences are those that involve being together: embracing, kissing our lover's neck, lips, and eyes, caressing, sharing intimate thoughts, giggling, being silly, massaging, learning to be completely relaxed, and accepting each other's unique, beautiful self. When warmed with the blanket of love, physical intimacy temporarily dissolves boundaries and merges two individuals.

Pre-marital sexual intimacy in adults is a matter of personal choice. Those who prefer waiting until marriage to be sexually expressive should be respected. Those who wish to explore the art of sexual love while single need not be lectured. Each person needs to follow the path most comfortable to him or her. It's best we avoid making the mistake of imposing our morality on those who have a different set of values. One of the principle causes of disharmony between groups is rigid adherence to moral or social doctrines that are presumed 'better' or 'nobler' than those of another group.

Those who wish to explore their sexuality need not apologize or feel guilty for being sexually attracted to other human beings and wishing to physically bond. Sex is natural. There is nothing wrong with adults having pre-marital physical relations as long as it is with mutual consent, and care is taken not to transmit infections or cause unwanted pregnancy. Healthy fulfillment of sexual desire releases pent-up tension and improves well being. If two individuals share their bodies in a mutually satisfying manner, they create happiness. There is no rational argument that it is not the proper thing to do. *People who live in glass houses should not throw orgies.*

Have you ever had a magical night with a lover and the next day you were so content you flashed a *life is so wonderful* smile at everyone? In the overview, I discussed that increasing our happiness will naturally spill over and have a positive ripple effect on those around us. Conversely, lack of fulfillment of this desire is a recipe for melancholy and may be followed by frustration and bitterness. The inability to properly concentrate on work, creativity, or other activities is a further consequence of an unsatisfied sexual urge.

Our desires should not distort and limit our ability to relate to others. Individuals exclusively dominated by sexual desire relate to attractive bodies as objects for self-gratification, neglecting all the wonderful inner qualities that people have. They miss meaningful connections.

Sexual intimacy, as with any art form, is a learning process— there's much to explore and experience. It would be unreasonable to expect the heavens to fall, the earth to shake, and lightning bolts to crash during our very first step into the beautiful sexual landscape. If your first experience was not satisfying, don't despair. Finding a partner with whom you feel completely comfortable may be the answer. Learning the art of sexual love takes time. We can't expect to be expert swimmers the first time entering a pool.

Masturbation, a perfectly natural method of stimulating oneself, is neither a sin, a perversion, nor a cause of health problems. The ability to be sensual and physically intimate with oneself is essential to being comfortable and open with a lover or spouse. "The next time you feel the desire (to masturbate) coming on, don't give way to it. If you have the chance, just wash your parts in cold water and cool them down," advised Robert Baden-Powell (1857-1941), the British General and founder of Boy Scouts. Aren't you glad he wasn't your father?

Homosexuality, lesbianism, and *bisexuality* are natural. If you are attracted to a member of your own sex, or both sexes, there is no reason for you to feel uneasy. Each person on this earth attempts to find his or her best way to nurture a sense of physical connection.

Next, we'll discuss romantic love and learn some of its secrets. Unlike self- and universal love, which provide a smooth and consistent ride, romance is a Ferris wheel of emotions. Once we board it, we can expect to go up and down, probably more than once. What a delight going up! However, if we ignore cultivating self- and universal love, relying completely on romance for our happiness, we take a risk. Falling in love is certainly one of the most thrilling feelings in life. The adoration from our lover makes us feel wonderful about ourselves– enhancing our self-love.

A failed romantic relationship similarly gushes forth emotions, but on the opposite end of the spectrum. *We cannot fully predict or control how our partner will feel about us in the future.* Nor can we fully predict how we ourselves will feel about our partner. A significant number of people in our culture believe that true life-long happiness lies in romance and marriage. It can. Sadly, just as often, a failed romance or marriage devastates people. When we exclusively depend on romance for fulfillment, we are unlikely to achieve consistent life-long happiness. In order for romance to be a reliable source of happiness, it needs to be built on a bedrock of self- and universal love. Consequently, one can use all three types of love in a synergistic fashion, magnifying each's heart opening potential. Romance enhances self-love. Enhanced self-love can in turn be harnessed to expand universal love. If the adoration shared with our partner is interrupted, we still have our intact selves to fall back on. The bedrock is strengthened even more when the other essentials in this book are addressed.

I'd like to relay to you a personal story, and if I may, engage full poetic liberty.

Romantic Love

My heart was warmed by Cupid's visit during my first semester at Drexel University in Philadelphia. I was in the library studying Erikson's stages of development when Aubrey, whom I had met in Psychology 101, came and sat across from me. With whispers and hushed tones, we began a trusting exchange of private thoughts revealing our mutual attraction. Soon, a natural radiance brightened our faces as our legs spontaneously interlocked under the table. I will always remember the moment as we faced each other when she reached with her left hand to touch my right hand, turned it over and outlined a heart on my palm with her red *Bic* pen, sending my heart into an urgent knocking at my ribs. Our eyes met as a teardrop swelled and cautiously coursed past her cream-white, young cheek.

Treasured are the times when Romance breezes through our hearts and chooses to pause a while. She is unlike any guest we have ever hosted before, for upon her welcome she assumes instant sovereignty
shatters the armor of composure
takes judgment prisoner
reverses all rules
passion precedes prudence
impulse before intellect
  while her bliss...
  her bliss of unchained ecstasy
permeates every pore
seeps into our souls
melts moments into infinity.

Autumn, auburn autumn, was never more sublime than the following few weeks of our passion. Her presence pervaded every moment of day and night. We spent long Saturday afternoons in the third-floor attic room of her parent's Victorian house. Windows spanned a view of a spacious backyard sprinkled with fallen oak tree leaves of crimson and gold. School work took a distant third place behind exploring bodies and listening to records. (The Moody Blues' *Days of Future Passed* and Simon and Garfunkel's *Sounds of Silence* were two of her favorites.) For the first time in my life, there was someone who encouraged and genuinely listened to all my private thoughts and secrets, accepting them without judgment. "I love the real you, the little Ray, way inside," she murmured one evening. My self-love swelled. During a December ski trip to the Pocono Mountains, we were in the back seat of the school bus in total embrace, oblivious to the stares of the other students, when a strong conviction arose. She was the perfect woman for me, my marriage partner.

We all wish Romance to stay forever, yet sadly she rarely fashions a permanent abode. Her nature is transient, a capricious squatter. In due time she may quietly bundle her charm potions, preen her feathers, wish us adieu, and flutter away. Or when she has lodged herself securely within us, she may abruptly escape from our partner's heart, quenching the raging flames of desire that once glowed our lover's gaze.

> Ice crystals
> hug crevices
> of cobbled streets.
> Liberty Bell greets
> New Year's festive eve.
> Your gloved grasp was weak
> a passionless stare into the night...
>
> Seated on the icy steps of Independence Hall
> brownstone shadow by
> faded street lamp
> huddled in my parka
> shivering
>   dazed

thoughts scattered as
school notes tossed
into a winter storm
lonely heart spiked
by ice pick of steel
halfway down the block
your silhouette paused.
I couldn't tell
　　did you look back?

Her intense passion was cooling. Even though we had a good relationship, she could sense that we were not marriage compatible. Outside
of our mutual amorous attraction, she believed we had few similarities.
I was too blinded by Cupid to notice. On the steps of Independence Hall
I promised I'd change, pleading, "I'll be anything you want me to be."
Eyes low, she shook her head. "Marry me or the relationship is over," I
foolishly gambled. She turned and walked away.

The 'winter semester of my discontent' began. I could hardly study.
Her mirage floated onto textbook pages, test answer sheets, and the
blackboard– unerasable. Amber-toned memories of autumn bliss replayed
in my thoughts like a compact disc that, having reached the end song,
continually starts anew.

*Precious is nurturing self-love before boarding romance's magic car-
pet ride. Just as a circus acrobat spins fearlessly in the presence of a safety net below, our love for self emboldens us to soar ever higher on love's
ethereal wings. For if or when the magic carpet is withdrawn and the
person we adore waves good-bye, our self-love spreads the net that catch-
es our bruised ego before its crash, dries the tears, tenderly
balms the wounds
carved by Cupid's cruel arrow
as it pierces the heart
twists a turn or two
and travels onward to its next target.*

Despite my initial abysmal distress my rational mind eventually reclaimed some lost ground. My self-love had received a setback but not been defeated. We were able to manage a friendship, albeit distant. Shortly after the breakup she moved to Taos, New Mexico. We corresponded intermittently– I read and reread each of her letters to find words or clues hinting of any interest to resume a love relationship. We saw each other when she came to Philadelphia on holidays to call on her parents. I felt an irresistible fervor at each of our encounters.

Countless heartbeats pulsed and passed; semesters came and semesters passed. After three years my passion began to slowly dissipate. Romance had loosened her grasp. During one of her visits, as we sat across from each other at a café on Spruce Street– my elbows resting on the wooden table with cinnamon tea cupped between my hands, the vapor warming my nose– I looked at her pensively, finally free of love's blinds. I pondered… our ideals and values *are* truly different. She was wise not to succumb to my marriage pleas.

Aubrey opened my heart and taught me how to feel. I matured into a deeper person. I will forever be grateful to her. Cupid's arrow wasn't so cruel after all.

Romance: how to create, nurture, dissolve… and cross your fingers, perhaps the stars in heaven will chime their nuptial bells

Self-love emboldens us to approach someone we find interesting. By taking the initiative of saying hello and being open, we tap the first domino in a series leading us to the captivating stare of chemical magic. The person we are attracted to needs to know that we are interested, even if it is in a most subtle way. Maybe the person you like is also interested in you but is nervous about letting you know. Your approach may take many forms; there is no single recipe or formula. Each interaction is unique with its own special key unlocking a dormant heart's barricaded gates. A catalyst in one situation may not work for another. Approach with a sincere attitude, open to all possibilities, truly believing that love transcends physical appearance, color, ethnicity, age, and social status. *A smile, a lingering glance, and a little bit of assertiveness have sparked many romances.*

Widen your possibilities of meeting potential lovers by joining various organizations, outdoor groups, athletic clubs, theater groups, and volunteer organizations. Make a variety of friends so you can meet their friends. Staying indoors, folding your arms, and hoping for that certain someone to call is not the best approach. Be relaxed, lead a low-stress life, and make yourself open to new adventures. Vacations are a great time to fall in love, especially if the setting is exotic. The second time I fell in love was with a Belgian woman while vacationing on the island of Guadeloupe in the Caribbean. Lead a complete and happy life, and when you exude positivity people will naturally be attracted to you.

Nurturing romance requires placing no demands or expectations, accepting whatever our lover wishes to give or share, communicating openly and honestly, appreciating and being grateful every day that romance cherishes us with her presence, and promoting a non-manipulative attitude. Say "no" to the *now that I've conquered you I can toy with you as a cat having cornered a little mouse* game. Spontaneity, such as an *I think of you all day long* cable or note, an unexpected bouquet of hand picked daisies and marigolds, a small personally made gift or artwork (drawing, sculpture) or other 'trivial' gestures, do wonders in keeping the enthusiasm of the relationship bubbling.

When romance begins to bundle her potions and signals she may soon fly away, our lover would appreciate the early warning. We owe our partner open and honest communication. It is unfair to avoid the issue by not returning phone calls, canceling dates at the last minute, or worse, not showing up at prearranged meeting places.

If we accept the possibility of romance's impermanent nature, we are more likely to part amicably without blame when the relationship is no longer satisfying. When two self-confident individuals dissolve a romantic passion the separation will lack the heart-wrenching distress that is common when the two are dependent on each other for their entire self-identity and happiness. These two mature individuals will hug, thank each other for sharing a wonderful time together and will move on, holding no regrets. If both partners have been honest and fair with each other, why not continue the friendship?

49

When passing through the doldrums of a romantic separation, keep in mind that the gloom will not go on forever. Loneliness is temporary. If your self-love was boosted by your lover's adoration, try to maintain it. You will overcome the sadness more quickly if you make the effort to channel your thoughts into self-improvement, find meaningful goals to pursue, widen your social circle, develop more intimate friendships, and keep in mind that there are an infinite number of potential romances circling around you. All that is necessary is to drop preconceptions of the exact height, weight, hair color, and ethnicity that you're seeking in a lover.

Let's spend a moment and pry open romance's kiss-sealed letter, unfold the enigmatic note within, and try to decipher the cryptic contents. *Is love chemistry?*

As discussed in the overview, our thoughts and feelings are due to communication between neurons. This communication is accomplished through chemicals called neurotransmitters. 'Falling in love' is linked to neurotransmitters released into certain parts of the brain. These neurotransmitters are in the same class as the amphetamines (stimulants). Scientists believe that the specific chemicals involved in romance may be *phenylethylamine, norepinephrine,* and possibly other neurotransmitters. When we initially 'fall in love,' these chemicals are released, race through our neuronal networks and ring a euphoric wake-up call. "The day has come, comrades! Sound the alarms, switch on the lights, pour out the hormones, prime the chemical pumps. Hum and drum the joy-song of Love!" As these chemicals reach our organs, hearts race, palms sweat, and lungs heave.

An accurate– but unromantic– translation of "I'm in love" may be: "Seeing you or thinking of you stimulates and releases pleasurable amphetamine-type neurotransmitters within my neuronal synapses– inducing ecstasy and irrational behavior."

Unfortunately, after a few months or years, the brain either releases fewer of these chemicals or develops a tolerance to the chemically-induced euphoria (most commonly two to three years). My case fit the norm– my passion dissipated at the end of three years. Aubrey's passion lasted only a few months. It is common for the brain to develop a tolerance to certain chemicals. Anyone who has taken sleeping pills or pain medicines for prolonged periods has experienced this type of tolerance. Higher and higher doses are needed to achieve the same effect. Tolerance to these love chemicals may signal the end of the romance.

Aware of this knowledge we can take certain steps to prevent disappointment and maintain healthier partnerships. Once we commit to a partner and decide to tie the knot, we can begin nurturing a more mature relationship based on respect and open communication. We culture a mature love that may be partly due to *endorphin* release (the chemical suspected in runner's high) and the hormone *oxytocin*. Endorphins have the potential to last much longer than amphetamines, even a lifetime, without the body building a tolerance to them. When passion begins to dissipate, we are protected by mature love, a calmer, more peaceful emotion. If ever our partner tells us, "You know, I don't get that *heart pounding feeling* when I'm with you anymore," we realize it's natural. There's nothing wrong with us or our partner. That's just the nature of romance.

Some scientists hypothesize that romance may be nature's way to keep a couple together after procreation and provide parental security until the offspring have passed through vulnerable infancy. It is interesting that romantic passion, on the average, lasts two to three years; the median length of marriages is four years. Is there a correlation?

Oxytocin is a hormone released by the pituitary gland. It is popularly known as the 'cuddle chemical' or the 'motherly love hormone.' The release of oxytocin occurs during orgasm, breast stimulation, and during childbirth when the baby is passing through the mother's vagina. A large dose of oxytocin causes sleepiness. (Now you know why your partner rolls over and starts snoring.) Oxytocin can produce feelings of satisfaction, attachment, and the urge to cuddle. In animal studies, species that had a greater number of oxytocin receptors in their brains were more likely to stay monogamous and bond more deeply with their offspring.

The study of love's chemistry is still in its infancy. Could self- and universal love be due to endorphins, serotonin, other neurotransmitters, or some combination including changes in neural pathways? More research is needed.

At this point some of you may be wondering, "What about the intangible part of romance– the magic. Is love purely chemical?"

Yes, say many scientists. Feelings and thoughts are due to friendly molecules getting along with each other... connecting, cuddling, and letting go. The complexity of the interactions is overwhelming. A healthy functioning brain made of 100 billion neurons harmoniously communicating with each other through neurotransmitters, electrical signals, peptides, and hormones... further communicating with the trillions of cells in the rest of the body while continuously adapting to the external world... is enough to impress me. *If anything is magic, the human brain is.* Humans have an incredible potential to feel euphoria, bliss, ecstasy. I speak from personal experience. Romance is not the only path to these heightened states. By taking a complete approach to becoming your best– satisfying the essentials in this book– these heightened states will visit and stay with you more often.

This is the science of love. More will be known in the coming years. Now let's drift back into the celestial clouds of poetry. What if Fortune smiles and mature love grows and sparkles in both partners?

> *Supposing the stars in heaven*
> *twinkle and wink;*
> *and the moon, content*
> *nods in assent*
> *whispering*
> *"Chime your bells little stars*
> *consent;*
> *let Love mature*
> *let her link*
> *this committed pair*
> *as they destine..."*

Marriage

"Love one another and make not a bond of love... Let there be spaces in your togetherness– let the winds of the heavens dance between you as the strings of a lute are alone though they quiver with the same music. And stand together, yet not too near together: For the pillars of the temple stand apart, and the oak tree and the cypress grow not in each other's shadow." Khalil Gibran, *The Prophet*

Marriage has the potential to be one of life's most satisfying experiences, a true connection between two individuals, creating ever deeper levels of commitment and communication. Marriage is a sharing of hope and vision, a synergistic bonding of body and purpose, and for many a joint venture in procreating and raising a vulnerable infant into adulthood. Fortunate is the person who finds a companion compatible romantically, sexually, and intellectually.

Unfortunately, for some, the married state may sadly spiral into disappointment. The dream, the long held fantasy, evaporates. Although hopes were high, the years do not unfold their promise as expected. What went wrong? Where did we fail? We were *one at heart*. We swore *till death do us part*.

We rarely fall in love and marry a real person. Instead, we are infatuated with a projection of what a loved one should be, a fantasy shrouded by magic and mystery. With the passing of seasons the veil unravels and we come to realize that this 'ideal person' has values, needs, and expectations different than our own. At this point the gong strikes and we awaken from our half-dream state.

Let's have realistic expectations. Sometimes people marry thinking they are in love, but the emotion felt as love may actually be something else: a strong sexual attraction, the security of being with another person, or the comfort of feeling approved. Conjugality needs to be entered cautiously (perhaps as cautiously as choosing to dash ahead of the raging bulls during the annual bull run festivities in the narrow streets of Pamplona, Spain). Disappointment is likely if cautious optimism is set aside in favor of the following unreasonable expectations:

> I don't know what to do with my days. Maybe marriage will miraculously transform my life into an enchanting experience. My partner and I will grow and mature at the same rate and in the same direction. Since love transcends disputes, we will not annoy each other or have fights. Our tastes in china, furniture design, and wallpaper pattern will be practically identical. Although my spouse is not exactly the type I'm looking for, I can mold him/her after we're married. Soon after the exchange of rings, the *weekend couch potatoing* in front of the tube and the *shopping mall marathon spending sprees* will cease.

Our romance will endure forever... our orgiastic passion will keep the neighbors awake as each night will find us locked in each other's embrace, lounged in overstuffed sofas, sipping brandy from each other's snifter, the flickering flames in the fireplace reflected in our shimmering eyes, taking turns reading from Elizabeth Barrett Browning's *Sonnets from the Portuguese,* "How do I love thee? Let me count the ways..." and yes, of course, Ravel's *Bolero* pulsing in the background. We will have beautiful children– models of perfect behavior, and a source of pride and joy.

Expectations must be discussed openly before hiring a photographer, ordering bouquets, and mailing invitations. When and how many children does each partner wish? What career goals does each person have? Should one member stay home while the other one works? How much freedom to do 'one's own thing' is presumed? What about money? Is one person a 'saver' while the other is a 'spender?' There are a number of important issues to deliberate. If you discuss these issues thoroughly, the odds for later disappointment are markedly reduced.

"Deceive not thyself by over expecting happiness in the married state," advised Thomas Fuller (1608-1661), the British writer. "Remember the nightingales which sing only some months in the spring, but commonly are silent when they have hatched their eggs." The key word is 'over.' Of course, we all marry or wish to marry in order to become happier. We certainly improve the odds of a blissful matrimony by becoming happier before we are married. Thereafter, marriage can make our lives even more special if we find the right person, plan appropriately, and continue putting effort into the relationship. Marriage is hard work. Continuing the relationship on a high note requires creativity.

Marriage does not always conform to childhood fantasies. Some marriages are blissful; others slide downhill. A significant number of couples stay together or tolerate their nonchalant relationship due to societal pressures, for the sake of the children, or to avoid the fear of living alone. As a family physician I have seen too many idealistic unions between wide-eyed, love-intoxicated young adults untied not long after matrimony. I have empathized with too many women and men overwhelmed by single motherhood or fatherhood. Some are poverty stricken, surviving on alimony, or paying out alimony, while they endure the responsibilities of working full-time and raising infants. They have little clue who they are or what they want to accomplish in life. Many of these young adults had their self-concept completely based on their marital state. When that's taken away from them, they crash. Susan B. Anthony (1820-1906), the American suffragist, counseled, "Marriage, to women as to men, must be a luxury, not a necessity; an incident of life, not all of it." Well, perhaps it's not merely an incident, but her point is that our whole self-identity should not be based exclusively on matrimony. Marriage is icing on the cake. Each of us, of course, is 'the cake.'

After the romance wanes, a couple has a better chance to stay together, happy and fulfilled, if they work together to develop a mature companionship, facilitated by open communication. Continued open communication is indispensable. As important as communication is a strong sense of respect and commitment. A commitment to stay bonded even through the low points of the relationship. In the long run, commitment is more important than romance for the survival of marriage, since commitment endures. Marriages last longer in cultures where romance takes a secondary role to commitment. Culturing a mature type of love is essential for the marriage to be satisfying.

A successful marriage also requires compromise. Flexibility is indispensable in order to accommodate the myriad decisions that constantly arise. These include the trivial, such as which corner to place the potted geranium, or decisions with more significant consequences. Public or private school for the kids? To buy a house or rent? It's amazing how even trivial disagreements can promote disputes.

As in a romantic relationship, in order to keep the passion burning longer, spontaneity and attention to detail are essential. Bring a rose home on a whim. Plan a getaway weekend by a lake or beach. Trade a massage by the fireplace. It's possible that weeks and months may pass without a couple having a deep conversation. Instead, trivialities of daily family life are discussed. A weekend out of familiar surroundings is a good opportunity to share whatever is on one's mind. Open up to each other all unexpressed thoughts and feelings. Choose to forgive your partner for past minor or major hurts, misunderstandings, and harsh words spoken during periods of stress. These hurts are common in all long-term relationships. Erase the slate where you keep a count of your grudges. It feels wonderful to begin again with a clean slate, this time keeping a count of all the positive aspects of the relationship.

Spouses are not to be taken for granted. We tend to compliment and flatter strangers, and rarely think about complementing our loved ones. We neglect to address them in the same respectful tone of voice as we do others. Maintain the respect and warmth you showed during the early days of the courtship.

When marriage lasts for decades, the partnership rooted in a lifetime of support, affection, sharing of common experiences, and roller-coaster adventures provides a wonderful sense of fulfillment and happiness. Slipping on the ring may be life's most significant single resolution. Let's be wise and walk to the matrimonial altar with the careful steps of a well thought out decision. We cannot fully predict what fanciful adventures, mysteries, or dark clouds may mushroom from three simple letters... *i*... *d*... *o*... but our prudent decision will defy the statistician's dire prediction. As my friend Lou affirms, "We then proceed knowingly into the unknown."

Choosing a spouse

If we become the type of person we want to marry and live with, our chances of finding an appropriate partner improve. The criteria in a partner necessary for successful matrimony are different from those involved in romance. Marriage is a serious, life-long matter. For the sake of long-term happiness, it is essential to find a dependable mate who is not only compatible sexually and romantically (a short-term necessity), but a friend and interesting conversational companion. To test whether a mate is truly compatible in the long run, ask yourself: if no sex or romance were involved in the relationship, would I still have a loving friendship with this person? Do I enjoy talking to him or her? If your answer is *Yes! Yes!* you have found *a* right person. If you haven't yet found this loving friend, wait. Staying single is preferable to having an unfulfilled marriage, a dysfunctional family, traumatized children, and possibly an acrimonious divorce. Romance and sex are not enough to keep a married household together forever.

The likelihood for a successful marriage can be enhanced by courting a good dose of realism and delaying the leap (into rapture, apathy, or the pits) until we grow wiser, more mature, and find the appropriate mate– a loving partner with whom we can grow, individually and together. Let's not choose our companion when we are too insecure, too young, and too naive to know which path we are to travel on this earth. Let's not choose our companion when we are still a pawn in life's continuing chess game. Let's first grow in wisdom and maturity, raise ourselves up to be a king or queen, then mate a winning partnership.

Sex and marriage

Sexual intimacy has the potential to flourish with marriage as the union becomes forged and formalized. A committed couple may grow to be completely open and communicate on an ever embracing level of physical bonding, melting at night into each other's arms, bare bodies braided, as a moonbeam peeps through the blinds finding her leg crossed over his hip.

On the other hand, if we marry young, before getting in touch with our entire sexual being and identity, and before fulfilling our desire to experience intimacy with different partners, marriage may become no less than a captive state. We may find ourselves caged, looking longingly through the bars at Temptation belly-dancing its seductive allure.

Once married, we relinquish the freedom of having guiltless sexual relations with different partners forever (or until a divorce). The reality and seriousness of this limitation may not sink in until years later. Before we tie the knot, the following are questions to consider: "Do I want this person to be my only sexual partner the rest of my life?" "Have I satisfied my need to be sexually adventurous?" "Am I comfortable with my own sexual preferences?" "Am I willing to be forever faithful?"

No matter how much we are sexually infatuated with someone before marriage, it is possible that boredom may eventually blanket the bedroom– while libidos are bundled and stored in the attic trunk. Compare it to eating chocolate ice cream every day. Eventually, taste buds habituate to chocolate and crave vanilla, strawberry, double-brownie nut or heavenly hash.

Even if our married sex life is satisfying– chocolate remains delicious– we may still have the urge to physically connect with others. Like the majority of mammals (only 3% of mammals couple with just one mate in their lifetime), humans are not by nature satisfied with one sexual partner. Anthropologic and sociologic studies show that being married to one partner is a natural human urge, but being satisfied with one sexual partner is not natural. This is attested by the substantial rate of extramarital affairs or at least the secret unfulfilled craving for an affair. Extramarital affairs have occurred throughout history in practically all cultures, no matter how severe the punishment– including ostracism, torture, or death. Humans habituate to the same sexual stimulus and seek variety. Could habituation be an evolutionary strategy to maximize the number of progeny and the continued survival of the species? It has obviously worked well– too well.

The married state, with its demands of faithfulness, may be a struggle to adhere to unless a couple continually creates stimulating games and complexities in each other's sexual company. Some couples successfully accommodate to habituation by mutually agreeing to have an 'open' marriage.

The cooling of the sexual passion in a long-term relationship is not the end of the world. The profound bonding, love, open communication, the sharing of the responsibilities in raising children, the daily exchange of stories… are all nourishing enough to supplant the vanishing sexual relationship. Many couples contentedly accept this inevitability. After all, there are more satisfying aspects to a relationship than sex (… oops, did I just type this? A jury of hormone-primed teenagers may sentence me to a firing squad for this blurt).

Those who are single, having read so far, may wonder whether to ever get married. Don't expect help from Socrates (470-399 BCE), the Greek philosopher. "As to marriage or celibacy," he observed, "Let a man and woman take which course they may, they will be sure to repent."

And now, the consequences of procreation: the intrepid sperm swam through all the barriers, found the Fallopian tube, and dove headfirst into the unsuspecting *mother of all* Ovum.

Family and children

As with marriage, nurturing a family and raising children can be one of the most fulfilling experiences in life. There are few things more gratifying than the love and connection a parent feels for a naked newborn babe, curled in the crib, soundly asleep, quite helpless, entirely dependent for all forms of sustenance and survival.

Raising children allows us the excuse to play with all the toys we gave up as we got older. What a great way to enjoy these toys, sharing the fun with our own offspring! Children appreciate the time we spend with them and cherish these special memories years later. Buy educational toys. Make learning fun. Encourage them to create and invent their own games. Hold their tiny hand and walk with them at the zoo. Learn the names of animals, birds and their habitats. Share their excitement at being alive!

What a thrill to observe an infant's growth and development as it miraculously transforms from a curious child into an independent teenager. When parents skillfully share their guidance and wisdom, a child's potential for achievement is limitless. All children require an overabundance of love and affection. Otherwise, as adults, their starved hearts will endlessly crave nourishment from outside sources. The amount of love and parental approval we receive as children determines our basis for self-love. We are unlikely to fail if we follow Mister Rogers' comforting message to each child, "You are special and I accept you just the way you are."

Each child inherits a characteristic temperament (fussy, well-behaved; calm, irritable; impulsive, cautious). As parents we should not get frustrated by an infant's particular odd temperament. It is difficult to predict in the early months how a child will eventually turn out. Even if your infant or child presents a difficult behavioral problem, continue with your love and patience. Be optimistic about your child's potential. Difficult, headstrong babies quiet down. Restless or inattentive children may become good students. Your patience as a parent pays off. Each child is unique and requires a unique approach to rearing in order to develop his or her full potential.

Falling short of parental expectations may induce lack of self-esteem. Parents may mean well when they prompt a child to constantly do better, but it makes a child feel that he or she is never good enough to satisfy their wishes. In certain cases, parents who have not become fulfilled or accomplished themselves place an inordinate amount of pressure on their children to succeed. If the children do not succeed, a sense of inferiority is certain to follow. *In addition to providing unconditional love, one of the greatest responsibilities parents have for their children is to be happy and fulfilled themselves.* Children learn best from parents who are good role models. Father: "Get up son; when Lincoln was your age, do you know what he was doing?" Son: "No, dad, I don't. But I do know what he was doing when he was your age."

We cannot mold our children precisely the way we want them to be. Our responsibility is to congratulate their accomplishments no matter how minor, encourage and reward their good behavior, channel their endless energies into positive outlets, and provide a nurturing shelter where they can thrive and grow. Home is the place where they are loved unconditionally, a nest where their self-confidence grows as do their wing spans, a place from which they try out their formative short flights knowing full well that they can safely return for refuge under daddy and mommy's expanded wings. Eventually, they will have the courage to bundle their belongings and fly off into the sunset, majestic, proud, independent, confident that they can fly any distance, glide across any ridge or gorge, hold ground through gales, and even design their own nest for a new generation of healthy eggs.

We have no choice in choosing our parents or relatives. Sometimes they may be very different from us. As much as possible, it is best to preserve a good relationship with all of them. As adults we can cultivate nurturing relationships with our relatives and parents by forgiving any hurts carried from the past. Families and relatives are 'tribes' providing a strong sense of security and belonging. Count yourself fortunate if your family life was joyful and stimulating. Not everyone had this blessing. Many harbor an armada of emotions regarding their upbringing. These emotions range from tender devotion to bitter resentment.

Alas, not every child is nurtured in a bed of rose petals. The modern western nuclear family cannot claim consistent success in providing a warm, loving, and nourishing garden for childhood development. The easily impressionable child is dependent upon the personality and character of two individuals who may not have reached maturity and self-actualization before becoming parents. The young, sensitive sapling may be bruised, stunted, and defoliated even with the best intentions by parents who may have more skill in driving a car (after all, no one can drive without taking driver education classes) than guiding a priceless human life to adulthood.

Every child has enormous energy and drive. As we observe children at play we realize that the natural state of humans is to be energetic and happy. Somehow, by the time they are young adults, many have had their zest zapped from them. What has robbed many children and young adults of their *joie de vivre*? What slows down their progress towards being happier? Of expressing their full potential? Why are some youth ragged-sailed, down-masted, hull-holed, water-logged, and almost shipwrecked having barely left port?

Emotional wounds can be healed.

BE HAPPIER STARTING NOW

THREE

Healing the Wounds

Man is born free, yet everywhere he is in chains.
Jean Jacques Rousseau (1712-78)
French Philosopher

Henry is a thirty-seven year old journalist who suffers from occasional bouts of depression. He had a difficult childhood due to his alcoholic father who would periodically hit his mother and leave home for days at a time. He recounted with anguish a most embarrassing moment at his high school graduation when his drunken father yelled inappropriate comments during the ceremony. "That's Henry's dad" whispered through the aisles as the seated graduating students turned their heads. Henry wished the earth would open a deep gorge to swallow his shame. Understandably, he still harbors a great deal of resentment towards his father. Soon after this incident, his parents separated.

Cheryl, a twenty-nine year old curator at a local museum, recounts with guilt the abrupt way she left her fiancee and moved from Chicago to Los Angeles two weeks before the wedding. She realized that she wasn't ready for a permanent relationship and was going ahead with the plans due to parental and societal pressures. When she changed her mind days before the wedding, she didn't have the courage to face her fiance and instead left town. Furthermore, she did not return any of his calls or letters.

Linda, a twenty-two year old college student studying biology, came to my office with upper abdominal pains and was found to have a stomach ulcer. When I asked her about any stress in her life, she revealed that much of it came as a result of her jealousy. Her very attractive dormitory roommate is showered with attention from male students. Recently, a heartthrob opted to date her roommate instead.

63

David is a twenty year old literature major with panic attacks. He harbors deep wounds from his childhood and teenage years when schoolmates mimicked his stuttering.

Barbara is a fifty-eight year old accountant being treated for hives. During one of her visits, we started talking about her previous marriage and subsequent divorce, "It's been six years since the divorce, but I still have anger towards him. Sometimes I feel angry toward all men. It was a bitter separation."

Do you have personal wounds preventing your progress towards being happier? Did you grow up in a dysfunctional family? Are you angry at one or both of your parents? Do you feel guilty or shameful about past errors in judgment? Do negative emotions such as envy eat your insides? Are you holding grudges against anyone? Have you had traumatic relationships that left you bitter?

Each of us encounters difficult or hurtful events while growing up. For some, the hurts are minor and fade into insignificance. Others are less fortunate as they suffer the torments of physical, psychological, or sexual abuse. Consequences of these hurts include low self-esteem, anxiety, depression, fatigue, and a weakened immune system.

Some individuals cope with outbursts of anger or violence like volcanic bubbling magma that explodes periodically to release accumulated pressure. Repressed and unresolved hurts slow our progress towards a full and happy life. The higher consciousness of universal love cannot be felt while these hurts continue to occupy valuable heart space– like weeds overgrowing a garden plot.

The intent of this chapter is to identify and make you aware of any restrictions towards happiness you may wish to overcome. Hopefully, this awareness will be the first step on the road to healing the wounds.

Healing old hurts

There are many ways to approach the healing process. Open up to a trusted friend and confide your private thoughts. Opening up and confiding in someone you trust has a wonderful cathartic effect– as if a dam has been opened and the rising water in the reservoir released.

Many feel instantaneously better having expressed a hurt they have kept inside for years. Studies show immune function and health improve when people disclose long-held traumatic experiences. You may also consider the help of a caring psychotherapist, discussing your feelings with your spiritual teacher, or joining a self-help group. Writing thoughts in a notebook or diary has helped many. Another possibility is to approach the person (father, mother, sibling, relative, teacher) who caused the hurt. In a mature, nonthreatening way, tell them how you feel. A letter can be a safe way to start if the relationship is still too painful. No matter what response you receive, the ultimate goal is to forgive and go on with your life. Another option is to change your setting. Move away from the environment that constantly reminds you of your hurts. This may involve moving to a new dwelling or to a new city. Healing these life-accumulated hurts may not be easy for those who have suffered extraordinary traumas, but they can often be remedied with time.

In the meantime, admit you were hurt and are presently hurting. Accept it. Love yourself for feeling sad. Weep. Cry. Let go. Make peace with those closest to you. Assume you only have a short time to live. Throughout your life find ways for catharsis and have a healthy cry. Release unexpressed emotions accumulated while living in this sometimes harsh world.

It is also possible that we have hurt or acted insensitive toward others. We may regret missed opportunities such as never having told our parents or grandparents we love them before they died, not having resolved arguments with loved ones, or not helped someone in need. None of us can go through life without making mistakes. We'll continue making them, hopefully less frequently. As a physician I make hundreds of decisions a month involving patient care. I cannot always expect to be right. If I were to constantly ruminate and not forgive myself for any errors of judgment, I would go on the rest of my life paralyzed by guilt. Is there anything you regret or feel guilty about? Write your thoughts in a private journal. Nurse the wounds.

Have you perhaps judged yourself and others too harshly for past errors and shortcomings? After all, you cannot change the past, only your attitude. Try a different approach. Accept yourself and others. Treat all problems old and new as opportunities to grow in wisdom. Allow yourself to live happily and cruise on the breeze-swelled sails of love and bliss.

> *The keel is healed*
> *the mast righted*
> *the hull sealed*
> *sew on the sails*
> *and sail on, sail on*

Begin to forgive yourself. Guilt is a type of self-punishment that continuously reopens a wound instead of healing it. Unload any guilt or shame burdening you. Forgive yourself and silence the battlefield raging within. Perhaps you could apologize to anyone you've hurt thru a letter or telephone call. Make amends in any manner that is appropriate for your particular situation. Forgiving ourselves does not give us *carte blanche* to carelessly and thoughtlessly repeat the same type of mistakes. Cheryl may in the future learn to give proper warning before she decides to end a relationship. Hopefully we learn from prior errors in judgment.

Once you forgive yourself, it becomes easier to forgive others. Some are fortunate to have had wonderful parents. Some parents were not so wonderful. If you harbor any resentment towards them, this is as good a time as any to reevaluate. Whatever mistakes you feel your parents made in raising you, they most likely tried their best given their own upbringing. They were once children whose little hearts may have been pierced by the daggers of sharp words carelessly slung by unskilled parents. Perhaps they were deprived of love and proper guidance. Ask your mother and father about their childhood. Did they receive affection from their parents? Were they roughly punished? Did they have hardships growing up? Were they teased and ridiculed by schoolmates? A child's Jello-mind is sensitive, malleable. Each word can either hurt or heal, sadden or enliven, crush or inspire.

You may also wish to forgive your present partner, spouse, or lover for prior misunderstandings, damaging words, or other hurts that invariably accumulate during a long-term relationship.

Take a few moments to sit quietly in your room and meditate. Breath deeply and then exhale as slowly as you can. Once you feel you have relaxed enough, bring to your mind a hurtful event. Take a deep breath and slowly exhale this painful memory out of you.

Forgiving makes us more open to loving others. By doing so we pluck the weeds from our heart's garden to find fertile soil for sowing the seeds of love. Over the next few days or weeks forgive every person or institution who has hurt you and write "I forgive... (fill in the blank)."

If you wish, write the following affirmation on the wall above your bed and each night forgive someone before resting your head on the pillow. Once you forgive everyone, remove these words.

> I forgive *myself.*
> I forgive *everyone.*

There is no point to forever tumbling in self-perpetuating thorns and thistles, endlessly ruminating on past mistakes and heartaches. Sophocles (496-406 BCE), the wise Greek dramatist, remarked over two millennia ago, "The greatest griefs are those we cause ourselves." Repeatedly focusing and endlessly talking about upsetting events reinforces negative neural pathways in our brains. Once we have ventilated repressed emotions and learned to forgive, we are able to rise from our despairing knees, take our first step towards the land of new beginning, and reshape our present and future.

Unnecessary suffering is neither noble nor heroic. It drains the patience and compassion of those who care about us and alienates friends and family members who may tire of the constant complaining, melancholy, and hopeless attitude. Let's move on and divert our concentration on things that motivate, improve our mood, and make us a better person. These would be working toward goals, developing healthier relationships, travel, exercise, creativity, and helping others.

Rechanneling negativity

Negative thoughts and emotions deplete our energy. They urge us to wish misfortune on others instead of elevating our own condition. They also induce harmful health effects. Chronic anger and resentment trigger the release of chemicals that accelerate the process of plaque formation in the heart's arteries. They also interfere with the proper functioning of the immune system, increasing our susceptibility to infectious diseases. Some forms of cancer may be triggered or accelerated by chronic negative emotions.

Jealousy and *envy* often stem from a lack of self-love. Instead of deriving pleasure from what we already have and are capable of, they cause us to feel pain at what others have. Content people do not covet their neighbor's home, greener grass, or new car. They are satisfied with their own state of affairs and wish everyone else peace of mind. In order to overcome feelings of jealousy, we need to learn ways to elevate our own condition and love ourselves more.

Linda felt envious of her roommate who was more attractive. Unfortunately, we live in a society that overemphasizes the importance of physical appearance. A five billion dollar cosmetic industry, anorexia, bulimia, and infinite numbers of people on diets are clear indications. Most of us, especially if single, are influenced by how we look and how others view us. Studies have shown that attractive people rate themselves happier on mood surveys. Being noticed as sexually attractive makes people feel better, especially during the hormone-ruled years of youth. What can be done if we don't look like Venus or Adonis? First, we have to accept the fact that we are not born equal. Some individuals grow up in happy families; other families are dysfunctional. Some grow in luxury; others poverty. Some are genetically healthy; others ill. Not everyone is blessed with good looks. However, as we discussed in the previous chapter, self-love transcends outer appearance. There are many individuals (you may know some) who are attractive, but have poor self-esteem. Others are unattractive, but exude charisma and self-confidence, and truly love themselves. Each of us has to do the best with the cards we are dealt. Loving ourselves can motivate us to improve our looks by exercising, developing muscles and body symmetry, and eating healthy foods. These are all measures that also improve our sense of well-being. Some people enjoy using make-up and psychologically benefit from cosmetic surgery. Improving our looks makes us feel better about ourselves. This leads to a ripple effect on those whose lives we touch.

We can also change the way we view others by placing less importance on physical appearance while we interact with people. Instead of noticing height, weight, hair style, skin tone, and other external features, we can focus on the beautiful internal qualities within each person. As we change the way we view others, we change the way we view ourselves; and vice-versa.

Anger is a draining emotion that serves little benefit. While it is appropriate to have it pulse through our veins during times of great personal or social injustice, it's best we channel it towards a constructive solution instead of self-perpetuating rage. Constantly expressing anger makes one angrier, solidifying a hostile attitude. Vocal tone during an outburst influences the experience of anger. A fast and loud expression makes us angrier; a slow and soft expression reduces it. Anger churns and eats our insides, interfering with our productivity. Take a minute and try to bring to your mind someone whom you have anger towards. If no one comes to mind, congratulations! If one or many people come to your recollection, now is the perfect time to discard this harmful emotion. Why should anger occupy valuable brain space? Erase the part of your brain where you store this feeling. Why let anger constantly disturb our state of happiness? Why should it be part of our daily life? Our thoughts and emotions can be guided. We can choose to feel anger or wave good-bye to it, erasing it out of our mind's dictionary. By improving our attitude (see chapter one) we find fewer reasons to get mad.

Repeated positive stimuli reshape neural pathways, leading to better functioning brains. Once we start on the road to self-improvement by working towards passionate goals, gaining financial security, taking vacations, becoming healthier, and satisfying the other essentials discussed in this book, we notice that envy, anger, jealousy, old wounds, and all other draining emotions no longer dominate our thoughts. They have dissolved into nothingness. With time, as we progress towards more self-fulfillment, we find these emotions a foreign concept. As these distracting negative thought patterns and emotions are dismantled, a tremendous surge in intelligence, memory, and creativity occurs. Our brain can finally function at its full capability. Therefore...

Let us not tarry by
Wasting youth upon a furrowed
Brow of woe
Trudging along slow
Fettered by anger, hurts, and despair
(The shackles of past emotional sorrow)
'Til our terminal hour when hair
Takes the shade of snow
And the cold curtain of the night
Blackens bedside candle's
shivering last light.

Let's forgive, forget, and...

... shatter the chains holding us back from happiness and the full flowering expression of our potential as human beings. Proceeding free, unfettered, soaring, to...

FOUR

Setting Goals to Follow our Dreams

Nothing contributes so much to tranquilize
the mind as a steady purpose.
Mary Wollstonecraft Shelley (1797-1851)
English novelist; author of *Frankenstein*

I was in my sophomore year at Drexel University in Philadelphia studying business administration when I started having doubts. While I found this field interesting, it no longer held a passion for me. Instead, in my free time, I was devouring books and magazines on nutrition. A very difficult fork in my educational path had appeared: do I continue as a business major or pursue a degree in health or medicine?

I couldn't decide. I had come face-to-face with a question that we all grapple with: "What do I really want to do with the rest of my life?" My initial choice, business administration, was not well thought out. As a child and teenager, I had shown a natural talent in arithmetic and would win most *Monopoly* and chess games. I guessed that this qualified me to enter the business field. As a college student, I questioned my motives and expanded my self-understanding. The nagging question kept recurring, haunting my concentration. I didn't know it at the time, but I was about to embark on following my dreams.

I spent the summer between my sophomore and junior years withdrawn in the room I rented at a fraternity house on campus. Days and days were spent, sometimes without going out, thinking and thinking. During the eighth week of this introspective semi-isolation, a strong determination began to brew and bubble within me. As a Phoenix rising out of the ashes, I announced to my friends and family, "I've made up my mind!"

I immediately changed my major to nutrition science with the intention of applying to medical school. I concluded that the best course would be to follow my passion in the health field. Medicine appeared to be the ideal career. I could learn about health, be intellectually challenged, and also have an opportunity to directly help people. If I couldn't get accepted by a medical school, back-up options included doing research in a health related field or striving for a Ph.D. in nutrition.

In order to graduate on time and qualify for the Medical College Admission Test as a senior in the fall, it was required that I complete in my junior year all the science courses consisting of biology, physics, inorganic and organic chemistry, and calculus. I registered for five science courses per semester. For one year I completely withdrew from all social activities and studied almost every waking moment of the day. The rewards soon came. I received straight A's in each semester, a good score on the MCAT's, and in late fall of my senior year, six of the nine medical schools to which I had applied called for interviews.

That year was one of the most difficult, yet satisfying, periods of my life. I had a clear purpose and was making good progress towards my goal. Each good grade reinforced my determination. It didn't seem to matter that I hardly dated or that I studied even on my vacations. I remember during the middle of January of my senior year receiving a letter from Thomas Jefferson Medical School. My trembling fingers ripped open the seal and a card appeared with the following breath-stopping words, "We congratulate you on being chosen to enter the class of 1980..." The temperature was in the forties, but for a whole week I walked about campus in euphoric delirium– without a sweater or jacket. I was warmed by the inner glow of happiness.

We influence our own present and future. Jean Paul Sartre, (1905-1980), the French existentialist, explained in his book *Being and Nothingness,* "Man can will nothing unless he has first understood that he must count on no one but himself; that he is alone, abandoned on earth in the midst of his infinite responsibilities, without help, with no other aim than the one he sets himself, with no other destiny than the one he forges for himself on this earth." Sartre is referring to both the global destiny of humankind and the destiny of each individual human being.

This is a powerful quote. It places the responsibility of the present and future squarely on our shoulders. It scared me when I first read it. Once I overcame the initial fear, I realized how empowering and liberating it was. If we don't get off our butts and take action, nothing will get done. Nothing is pre-planned. If I didn't have the thought of writing this book and the self-guidance to bring it to fruition, you would not have been exposed to these ideas. I've passionately enjoyed creating this book. I'm forging a path into the unknown. I truly believe it came about as a result of *freewill*. It was never *meant* to be. Thomas Mann (1875-1955), the German novelist, believed the same. In *The Magic Mountain,* he wrote: "Human reason needs only to will more strongly than fate, and she *is* fate." It is up to us to seek and find our own goals and meaning in life, make the effort, and rely on no one but ourselves. If we do get help from family, friends, the government, or others, that's wonderful. Let's appreciate the help but not take it for granted.

Having this sense of control is crucial to health and happiness. From now on, genuinely believe that you can choose and influence the path of your life. Nothing has been pre-planned. Wake up each morning and decide to be happier and more loving– because you want to. Decide that you will improve yourself and work towards your full physical, intellectual, and emotional potential.

We have freewill. We can shape our present and future, become happier, and change the course of our lives and the lives of others by our thoughts and actions. Fortune will smile on you if you work hard, take initiative, and persist. As you create opportunities, you increase your chances of being in the right place at the right time. It will *seem* as if you are lucky; as if everything always goes right for you; as if there are pre-planned coincidences and synchronistic events helping you along. A person who does not take initiative to explore new options is unlikely to encounter life's infinite promises. *Opportunity is a lazy goddess who rarely comes knocking on our door. She prefers being pursued.*

Barring excessive genetic or environmental impediments, our happiness on earth is a direct result of using our willpower to maximize our potential. Happiness requires knowledge. The learning and implementation of this knowledge requires self-guidance. Ultimately, we are responsible for our own well-being.

Let's not underestimate our potential

Each of us has unique talents and interests. Few of us utilize our innate gifts. Fewer of us maximize them. Evolving, growing, and becoming our best is inseparable from a fulfilling life. We can be better in many ways than we are now through resolve and perseverance. Thoreau agreed in *Walden*, "I know of no more encouraging fact than the unquestionable ability of man to elevate his life by a conscious endeavor." We only use a portion of our physical, intellectual, and emotional potential.

When setting goals, view success as working towards and achieving your own potential rather than surpassing or defeating others. Take a few moments now to make a list of what you would like to strive toward in the next six months to a year. These could involve diet, exercise, career, relationships, finances, etc. Even goals you consider minor are acceptable. The important point is for the goal to be realistic and well-defined. Write down at least two goals. There is no point waiting for the New Year to make a resolution. The rest of your life begins at this moment.

Obtaining a sense of accomplishment from small goals gives us the confidence to proceed to greater ones. Achieving goals enhances our self-esteem and self-control. Now make a list of goals you would like to work towards within the next one to five years. These goals should be slightly more challenging. Write down at least one.

Now, think about what your lifelong goals are. Before setting these long-range goals, it's important to get in touch with your passion. Passion is an intense urge directed toward a certain objective. Is there anything that you daydream or frequently think about? If you had no responsibilities for a year, what would you want to do? What do you wish you had more time to do? If you know what your passions are, you are fortunate. If you don't know at the present, think, persist. Ask people you meet what they do. Keep your mind open and aware. Persist in plowing your mind's fields until a fertile soil is provided for seeds to sprout. It may take long periods of introspection. No one but you can find or create your passion. When you get a feeling of full absorption with an activity or purpose, you know you have found it. A sense of being intensely alive and completely fulfilled is an indication that this is what you were meant to do and be.

If life were compared to a movie, each of us would be our own writer, director and actor. Why not write, direct, and *experience* a script full of *more* happiness, love, and meaning? Which brings us to...

What is the meaning of life?

Since the dawn of intelligent thought, humankind has grappled with the question of life's ultimate meaning. Defining this for oneself can be a difficult challenge, but doing so significantly influences happiness. If you have a religion or belief system that already provides you with meaning, follow that path. If you are not certain about your meaning, read on.

Some philosophers believe that there is no inherent meaning to life, it is what we make of it. We mold a meaning, shape it, and continually refine and improve it. Each of us is a unique individual with different backgrounds, perspectives, beliefs, and goals. It follows, therefore, that we create different meanings in life that may change as we mature and grow wiser.

Our long-term goals are intertwined with what we perceive to be our life's meaning. Take a moment and write down your lifelong purpose or meaning at this point in your life. Place today's date next to it. If you are not sure, reflect on this over the next few days, weeks, or months. When you are ready, write it down at that time. Don't be upset if you write something down now and find that you want to do something different later. We are all dynamic beings, constantly growing and evolving. It's okay to change goals and meanings as we mature. *If you are trying to find meaning through outside sources and can't find it, create your own.*

When setting plans for the future, it is best to plan a succession of modest goals. Rather than shooting for the stars and landing in the basement, set goals that can be achieved realistically. As a rule, the best goals are those that provide a sense of competence through a series of small steps in the right direction. *All or nothing* gambles sometimes pay off, but it's unwise to put all your eggs in one basket. Optimism is helpful in achieving an objective.

Reaching a goal is often not as important as the feeling of satisfaction gained at every step along the way: making new friends, growing, and learning from each new experience. The view from a mountain top may be great, but there are times when the peak is cloudy or snowbound. 'Success,' wealth, and fame have been unkind to certain individuals (celebrities, politicians, royal family). There are just as many pleasant scenes along the trail up to the mountain top that we miss if our necks are constantly arched upwards. Goal-achievement is only one aspect of happiness. It is too dearly purchased if all the other ingredients (health, love, and friendship) have been sacrificed in order to obtain it.

Postponing short-term pleasure is acceptable if it leads to long-term satisfaction. Consider it an investment to make short-term sacrifices in order to reap future rewards.

If unable to achieve a goal with a great deal of effort, reevaluate. Perhaps your skills and talents lie elsewhere. This presents a difficult decision. Is it best to persist on that path or choose another? Persistence may lead to rewards. Other times you may be casting your net in fish-less ponds. Perhaps the goal was unrealistic. Consider an error in judgment an opportunity to reevaluate goals and redirect. Goals have to be realistically balanced with abilities. *If at first you don't succeed, give up sky diving.*

It is never too late to set about doing what makes us happy. Pablo Casals (1876-1973), the noted cellist, continued playing and conducting orchestras up to his death at age ninety-six. Grandma Moses (1860-1961) was a farmer's wife and taught herself painting. She started her art work at age sixty-seven! She painted innocent and colorful scenes from rural American life and lived to be a hundred and one. Jonas Salk (born in 1914), discoverer of the polio vaccine, is actively involved in HIV vaccine research. *No matter how old you are, pursue a goal as if you were to live forever.* As my brother advises, do the best you can, with the means you have, in whatever situation you find yourself.

What is the author's *Raison d'Etre?*

I believe I should rely on no one outside of myself to give meaning to my life. My life has no predetermined meaning. I have *created* and developed it on my own. I view it as an ongoing process that may change with time. I am thirty-seven. At this point in my life, my meaning is to continuously increase happiness for myself and others. I plan to follow my own advice written in these chapters, distribute this book, and teach. Also, I love to learn. I plan to continue acquiring knowledge from multiple disciplines, synthesize it with my personal insights, and share it with anyone who is interested.

We've done our best... now it's time for rest

Having completed a grueling four years in medical school and an exhausting, every few nights on call, residency program in family medicine, my relaxed stint as a cruise ship doctor in the Caribbean and Hawaii was invaluable in resetting my priorities and pace of life. My batteries recharged. Hence, after achieving a certain goal, it is wise to

lie back on a hammock
basking in palm shade repose
canopied by cantaloupe-orange sunset skies
savoring coconut milk sips
while luxuriating in a halcyon state
of lazy levitation...
tensions and cares y a w n e d
into the winged clouds
of ephemeral daydreams
that dissipate– swallowed
by horizon's endless expanse.

This is the time to truly slow down, toy with Epicurean thoughts, and tackle the intelligent pursuit of pleasure, placing our type A personality on pause.

Let's consider ourselves fortunate if we have found passionate goals. Wouldn't it be great if one of these passions happens to be our work?

BE HAPPIER STARTING NOW

FIVE

Finding Satisfying Work

Blessed are they who have found their work,
let them ask no other blessedness.
Thomas Carlyle (1795-1881), Scottish writer

"I can't wait to go back to my law firm," spoke Marge, a thirty-eight year old paralegal who fractured her right ankle falling down the steps on the way to the basement. Her injury required a cast and crutches for six weeks. "After three weeks, I'm getting bored stiff. I read Amy Tan's *The Joy Luck Club*, Waller's *The Bridges of Madison County*, saw two movies a day, and caught up with all my 'soaps.' My job is really stressful. I never thought I would miss it."

Thomas, a thirty year old film editor, sounded a similar story. While at work, a secretary slipped and spilled the contents of a boiling coffee pot on his buttocks. It seeped through his pants and caused palm-sized, second-degree burns on both cheeks. "Doc, when am I going to get to go back to work? I thought staying home all day and watching basketball on the sports channel would be a dream come true. After eight days I'm ready to hit the bottle."

Work is an overlooked factor in personal happiness. Although we are often looking for ways to *avoid* work, surveys show that people are more likely to get the 'blahs' on Sunday when there is little structure to the day. Hours go by inefficiently while people sleep late, become easily tired or lethargic, take midday naps, waste time, and ruminate on past events. Minds drift into chaos. As it happens, work is *essential* to happiness and fulfills many purposes. It is a source of income, provides the framework by which we structure our daily lives, and fosters the milieu wherein we develop our intellect, skills, and abilities. Work also provides an opportunity for community-building based on the shared goals and aspirations of colleagues. Due to the contrast it provides, work makes vacation and leisure time even more special.

Three years ago, I worked as an information desk volunteer on Tuesday evenings at the Santa Monica Youth Hostel. (Youth hostels provide inexpensive, overnight accommodations for travelers from all over the globe. The name 'youth' is a misnomer since a person of any age is welcome.) I answered questions about what to do and see in Los Angeles. I had the opportunity to meet and talk to visitors from dozens of countries. Most were on short trips to the US although there were some, especially Australians and New Zealanders, who would travel around the world for two to three years. After a few months of meeting and talking to many of these *Wanderjahr* travelers, I noticed a consistent pattern. Those who had been on the road for more than a year or so did not seem to be as excited and energetic about their continuing travels. Pierre, a blasé Frenchman from Nice, aired a common refrain, "I look many museums, they all the same. No?" Susan, a kiwi, born and raised on a sheep farm near Wellington, stated, "You've seen a few mountain chains, you've seen them all." Rarely did I come across people who had been on the road more than one year, yet were still thrilled to be seeing new sights. Many reported that they thought traveling could stay enjoyable forever. Now, they were ready to pack up their bags and go home to a daily routine and begin working again.

Along a similar vein, have you ever wondered why many extremely wealthy individuals continue working even though they have the option to retire and relax? An example is Bill Gates of Microsoft. Why wouldn't he cash in all his billions in exchange for a lifelong binge of hedonistic gratification? Work is satisfying to him, and possibly to other wealthy individuals who continue working. It is a game and something to enjoy. One may derive more satisfaction from work than from sensual pleasures. It's also possible that some of these people (workaholics) have not learned how to intelligently pursue pleasure.

Work is a source of income. Money is necessary for survival. Many of us would be bored without employment or jaded if overindulged in pleasure. Let's go about...

Finding our bliss through work

Discovering a satisfying career that is also financially rewarding will contribute *enormously* to long-term health and happiness. Work usually occupies close to half of our waking hours. Stress and frustration are certain consequences of an unpleasant job or career choice. Studies show that working at a satisfying job or absorbing task *promotes* health. The ideal career is one that challenges our intellect, stimulates the development of skills, provides a sense of accomplishment, autonomy, and control, and contributes to society. Doubly blessed are those whose work is consistent with their meaning in life.

For some, the search for that 'ideal' career may be one of life's most difficult challenges. Too often we are expected by the end of high school or college to know how to occupy our lives till retirement. Few of us know ourselves well enough so early; it may take months or years of treading various mazes and paths before a comfortable niche is found. Perseverance leads to rewards. It is worth the effort to find passionate work that absorbs us in hours of total creative concentration. A giant leap towards long-term happiness is made when work is found that ceases to be toil, but actually becomes play. Work can be something to look forward to, as well as something to enjoy.

Each of us is a unique individual with special talents and interests. Let's make the effort to find out who we are. Our self-image is strongly influenced by our work and career. One of the first questions people ask upon meeting is, "What do you do?" Many of us equate much of our self-identity with our occupation. Let's find something that we can be excited about– something that we are able to do with enthusiasm, passion, and love. A businessman must make deals, a scientist must invent... "A musician must make music, an artist must paint, a poet must write, if she or he is to be ultimately at peace with her/himself. What a woman and man can be, they must be," wrote Abraham Maslow (1908-1970), the American psychologist.

What if work gives you the blues? If your present work is not satisfying, the following suggestions can help guide you:

1. *Change your attitude.* Attempt to make the best of the work situation rather than find faults. Doing so can often make work bearable, if not enjoyable. There are many ways to do this: learn to focus on the positive aspects of your job and the people with whom you share a large part of the day. Be on good terms with co-workers and your boss. Congeniality is often as important as skills and knowledge for career advancement. Nurture friendships over conflicts. Appreciate that you *have* a job, especially during slow economic times.

I once worked with an emergency room physician who changed his job four times in three years. He was eager to explain his reasons. The first hospital had too much paperwork and red tape. The second had inadequate parking and lousy cafeteria food. The third had a nursing supervisor with whom he didn't get along. His present practice was also unsatisfying since the lab and x-ray results took too long. It was apparent that he was the type of person who would not find satisfaction anywhere he went. It wasn't the jobs that were the problem (few jobs are perfect, anyway), but his attitude.

As a teenager I spent a summer working in an optical company that manufactured glasses. There were ten employees and I got to know them well. I noticed a striking difference in work enjoyment among the workers. Marty wore a sour face and rarely had anything positive to say about the company. He frequently argued with co-workers and labored as slowly as possible. On the other hand, Louie smiled, whistled, and approached each lens grinding job as if he were creating a piece of art. Both of these individuals were doing the exact same work. Yet their attitudes determined their sense of work satisfaction.

We have greater control over how we view our jobs or careers than we think. One option is to look at it as if it were a chore, or an infringement on our freedom. Another perspective is to see it as a game, enjoy the immediate experience, and see the wonderful possibilities it offers for growth and productivity. Furthermore, we can appreciate how our work contributes to society, upon which we depend for survival.

The quality of our lives and the lives of others is enhanced if we smile, greet our co-workers and customers with enthusiasm, and work with love.

2. *Change the circumstances at work that are making things unpleasant.* There are times when you are unable to change your attitude. It may be appropriate to try to change the external circumstances that are affecting you.

Abby is a patient of mine who is an account manager at a large department store. She was being treated harshly by a boss who often yelled at her, constantly criticized her performance, and demanded projects to be completed within unreasonable deadlines. She would arrive home in the evening exhausted, and sometimes in tears. On her way to work in the morning, she often experienced headaches and feelings of nausea. Sometimes a panic attack would set in. After months of enduring this unpleasant condition, she finally decided to do something about it. She asked to have a private talk with him. In a non-threatening way she related her feelings. As it turned out, he had not been aware that his behavior was affecting her in such a manner. He learned to treat her with more respect.

There are occasions when neither a change in attitude nor a change in work environment are possible. A discussion with a boss does not lead to a change in behavior. You do not find the job rewarding or stimulating. At this point you have the option to continue being distressed, or more productively…

3. *Look for other employment or change career goals.* This can be painful and scary. With perseverance and constant effort, greater dividends follow. It's not easy to make changes, especially if you have been working at the same place for a long time.

Robert, an engineer at a defense company for fourteen years, did not find satisfaction in working for a big corporation. He had many creative ideas that were too slow in being accepted by upper management. While at home in the evenings, he began working on one of his inventions, a part for an electric car. He gradually refined his invention and was able to get a contract from a car company to provide them with a supply of these parts. He quit his steady job and concentrated full-time on his new, self-started business. He is doing well and is much more fulfilled with his present self-employment.

4. *Work fewer hours.* Many jobs can be tolerated or even enjoyed if not done full-time. There is a great difference between working four days a week, with three days off, versus a regular five day work-week. Many jobs are inherently stressful; emergency room nurses and air traffic controllers are two. The extra day off contributes significantly to relaxation and provides the opportunity to pursue hobbies and other interests. The decrease in income may be offset by finding ways to spend less money.

Once we find the type of work that captivates our passion, wouldn't it be wonderful if it provided financial stability?

SIX

Being Financially Secure

*Money is like a sixth sense without which you cannot make
a complete use of the other five.*
William Somerset Maugham (1874-1965), English novelist

Our culture gives us mixed messages about money. We are advised from childhood that "money can't buy happiness." Yet we're constantly exposed to advertising that tells us we'd be happier if we purchased a new luxury car, a better stereo system, designer clothing, and a heavier-load washer/dryer. The media depict the wealthy having a wonderful time sunbathing in Acapulco or delighting their gourmet palates at five-star restaurants in Paris. Just how does money figure into happiness?

- Money, up to a certain point, *can* promote happiness. It provides a sense of security essential to well-being. However, a saturation point can be reached where additional wealth makes little or no difference in furthering a happy life. This is called "the law of diminishing returns." How much is enough? The level at which no further gains are made in promoting happiness is different for every individual.

- Lack of the adequate funds necessary to cover basic needs of survival and comfort is one of the most common sources of stress and discontent, interfering with a person's quality of life.

- Money can increase or decrease happiness depending on how wisely it is spent.

The old adage "money can't buy happiness" is not true. We need money to pay for food, lodging, transportation, and all the other essentials necessary for survival and comfort. Recreation and travel can certainly promote happiness and usually require money. Adequate funds enable us to purchase a car with a good engine that will not cause us problems. No longer need we occupy weekends clipping out coupons to save nickels on bathroom air fresheners and Grade AA Jumbo eggs.

Financial security is defined as "the point at which a person has enough savings or regular income to support a comfortable lifestyle." 'Comfortable' is different for every individual. Some need only a small amount of savings or earnings to support their simple lifestyle. For others, a large bank account or earnings is necessary for peace of mind. There are two ways of being rich: to have great wealth or to be content with what we already have. Once the basics of survival and reasonable comforts have been satisfied, our *attitude* regarding money is more important than the dollar amount of our financial portfolio. Those who know how to use money well in the promotion of happiness are better off than those who think they need more.

Being financially stable increases our options in life by allowing us the freedom to channel our energies toward self-growth and creativity. This stability makes it possible for us to enrich our lives by pursuing other interests, doing volunteer work, or starting philanthropic projects. It frees us from the drudgery of excessively working at a job we don't enjoy. We cannot concentrate on helping others or feeling universal love if we're preoccupied with how we're going to pay our bills. It's not easy to stay 'enlightened' without money. James Baldwin (1924-87), the American author, was blunt: "Money, it turned out, was exactly like sex. You thought of nothing else if you didn't have it, and thought of other things if you did." (From *Nobody Knows my Name*.)

Common sense advice on money management
Discipline yourself to save money. This is crucial in case of emergencies. The additional savings is a source of income through interest. Walter, a self-employed plumber, had the misfortune of having his van with all

his equipment stolen. It took four months for the insurance company to partially reimburse his loss. If he hadn't saved 30,000 dollars, which allowed him to return to work with a new van and tools, his income would have sludged to a halt.

Keep expenses low. In this age of credit cards, it is easy to run up debts without even realizing it. To simply extend a piece of plastic card and buy expensive clothes, furniture, or jewelry is denying the eventual reality of monthly bills. (Plastic surgery works wonders: *i.e.,* cutting across the middle of the card with a scalpel.) David and Sheila, a newly married couple, maxed out their credit card at the limit of ten thousand dollars by buying expensive furniture for their new apartment. Soon afterwards, he was laid off from work. They had to resell the furniture at a substantial loss.

Evaluate your budget regularly. Cut out fat. A friend of mine, a busy psychologist, was paying thirty-two dollars a month for cable TV, but hardly had time to watch. She reviewed her budget and realized that she was wasting 384 dollars a year. She stopped subscribing and has not missed the absence of cable.

Use extra caution when purchasing a house. Owning a house can be a rewarding experience but it may lead to sundry hassles that interfere with your peaceful state. When in the market for a new house, thoroughly inspect all angles before making the commitment to purchase. Do you have a guaranteed job that secures a steady future income? Are you planning to keep your house for at least five years? Have you considered the cost of homeowner's insurance, lawn maintenance, and the myriad other costs that are inherent to home ownership?

Before having and raising children, realize the expenses involved. It's unfair for children to be brought up in an environment where the lack of adequate finances interferes with the development of their full potential. According to the US Department of Agriculture, a child born in 1990 and raised until age eighteen will cost the parents, on the average, over 200,000 dollars. As Juvenal (50-130), the Roman poet, wrote nineteen centuries ago: "It is not easy for men and women to rise whose qualities are thwarted by poverty." Financial difficulties are a frequent cause of strife among couples and families.

It would be great if we lived in a world where we could constantly gratify pleasure, make love all day, help others, improve society, and pursue our passion without having to worry about money. In the 1960's, this experiment was partially tried through the "turn on, tune in, drop out" movement. The reality of finances was one of the obstacles that kept interfering with the maintenance of this higher consciousness. A better alternative is to *turn on, tune in* and *stay in*. There is no reason why we cannot be active, contributing members of society and still have a happy and meaningful life.

Possessions

Each of us owns an unimaginable number of objects. Throughout our lifetimes we accumulate clothes, gifts, books, photos, stuffed animals, CDs, newspaper articles, dishes, plants, furniture, and much more. With the passage of time objects take on sentimental value and become difficult to part with. The lime-green teddy bear resting on my stereo speaker holding a tiny American flag speaks of a carnival water gun contest won by a former love.

Keeping possessions to a minimum has many advantages. It allows for better organization, presenting less of an opportunity for loss or misplacement. This organization saves time and money, leading to greater opportunities for other pursuits. We don't have to let our possessions control us. Why not take Thoreau's advice, "Our life is frittered away by detail; *simplify, simplify.*" The acquisition and storage of material possessions rarely leads to long-term happiness.

Most of us can live a decade without purchasing any more clothes. We tend to amass so many possessions, yet like programmed robots we keep returning to the shopping center to recreationally consume more. Why is this? We are inundated by advertisements that overwhelm our judgment. Many people can't think of better ways to spend weekends than to walk up and down shopping malls. Is it an escape from loneliness? An opportunity to run into acquaintances? A quick way to temporarily raise our mood? If we find ways to better occupy our time, such as creating an art work, writing a letter, spending quality time with friends, playing games, taking outdoor hikes and trips, pursuing meaningful goals, etc., we won't be triggered by this thoughtless shopping reflex. A quote from Socrates (469-399 BCE), the Greek philosopher, comes to my mind when I'm browsing: "Often when looking at a mass of things for sale, he would say to himself, 'How many things I have no need of!'"

Once a year make an inventory of belongings and sell, discard, recycle, or give to charity objects that have outlived their usefulness. Unless it's special, if a piece of clothing has not been worn in the past three years it is safe to assume that it may not be worn again.

If you're planning to make an important purchase, whether it is a stereo system, a car, furniture, an appliance, etc., take the time to research and buy good quality. Read over the information available in *Consumer Reports,* ask friends who are knowledgeable. It costs more in the long run to purchase something of poor quality and then replace it a year or two later.

"Every increased possession loads us with a new weariness," noted John Ruskin (1819-1900), the English writer and social reformer. In the previous section on finances we briefly discussed that money can increase or decrease happiness depending on how wisely it is used. I once knew a stockbroker who had the life-long dream of owning a yacht. He finally amassed enough wealth to purchase a ninety footer. You should have heard the excitement in his voice when describing the beauty of his new acquisition. Every weekend he took the boat out to sea. During the following few months many of his weekends were spent tending the yacht, making repairs, fixing the engine, whitewashing the hull, and cleaning the sails. He soon became tired of all the maintenance and hired helpers to do the chores. In the meantime his wife was growing impatient. His time with her was shrinking. The expense of the yacht kept increasing as a new engine became necessary and part of the hull needed to be fixed when it collided with a sailboat. Arguments with his spouse became more common. Expenses kept mounting. The

October 1987 'Black Thursday' stock market crash dramatically reduced his income. He finally sold his yacht at a substantial loss and was able to mend his marriage. I had dinner with him the day he unloaded his yacht. He was all grins. He asked me, "Do you know the two happiest days of a man's life? The day he buys a yacht and the day he sells it." I remembered an observation by Pliny the Younger (61-112), a Roman administrator: "An object in possession seldom retains the same charm that it had in pursuit."

When our possessions possess us

I was five years old bouncing a tennis ball against the walls of my room when it took an unexpected hop crashing into an amber-hued clay pot given to me by my uncle who had just returned from a trip to Greece. The pot had a figure of a javelin thrower on one side and the Parthenon on the other. It now lay on the floor, shattered. I immediately burst into tears. My grandmother, who was baby-sitting, walked into the room to see what had happened. I told her how much the pot had meant to me. Now, it was all broken. She was wearing a below the knee, black and white, polka dot dress as she dried my tears with the hem. She sat down on my bed and calmed me with a fable.

> Once upon a time, a long time ago, there was a wealthy king who lived in the most beautiful castle. The walls were gilded with gold, his clothing was embroidered with silver. Rubies and diamonds gleamed from everywhere. Even with all his wealth and jewels, his most cherished possessions were three crystal vases from antiquity. They reflected sunlight in rainbow like patterns and were a joy to look at.
>
> One day, as the king was gazing at one of the vases, it slipped from his grasp, fell to the marble floor, and shattered into many fragments. The stunned king immediately summoned his aides and ordered them to find anyone who could mend the vase. Crystal workers from all over the empire came to the palace, but none could adequately put the vase back together. The king was dejected; he sulked daily and would isolate himself in his room, alone like in a tomb. One of his most prized possessions was smashed and no one could help. Counselors, dukes, princes, all tried to cheer him up, to no avail.

An old wise woman, having heard of the king's despair, limped to the palace on her cane. She asked to see the king because she claimed she had a cure. Was she a crystal worker? No. Then how could she solve the problem? Everyone was skeptical. Nevertheless, the king allowed the woman to propose her solution. What could be lost? She immediately proceeded to his chamber where the other vases were kept, raised her cane above her head, and swung as hard as she could, shattering the remaining two vases into fragments. Then she said, "Your highness, I'm sorry to have taken this drastic measure, but you have been a kind king to your subjects. We care about you. By breaking the other vases I hope to liberate you from basing your happiness on material goods. You have so many reasons to be happy. Appreciate your health and the love of your subjects. Look at nature and see how perfect it is. The same joy you derive from the vases is available in the rainbow-hued bubbling brook flowing next to your palace."

The king was shocked. He immediately had the guards escort her to prison and sat back in his chair, even more despaired than he was before. For days he cried and cried. Now all three of his vases were lost. Anyone trying to console him would be turned away... yet, her words kept coming back to him: *bubbling, nature, rainbow...* what did she mean by *the same joy*?

He looked up, and through his window, previously obscured by the vases, he could see, beyond the pasture, sunlight dancing on water. Drying his tears, he walked to the castle gate and asked that the portcullis be raised. He crossed the drawbridge spanning the moat and took a path through the bright-green meadow leading to the brook. Along the way the peasants greeted him with cheers, "Your Highness, we're so glad to see you again." "Your Highness, we missed you." The king waved back and kept walking. He sensed the beginning of a smile on his lips. He reached the brook, and... lo... the wise woman was right. There were endless rainbow-hued undulating patterns dancing all across the water. Swarms of fluorescent, sequin-like, shimmering minnows swam against the current. Each of the pebbles at the bottom of the brook was its own world full of myriad patterns. This brook-enchanted meadow was more fascinating than the vases ever could be!

At once, the wise woman was released from prison and became the king's trusted counselor. He shared much of his wealth with his subjects, and they all lived happily ever after.

When I watch scenes on the news showing fires flaming homes, flood-waters drowning farms and silos, hurricanes twisting off roofs, earth-quakes cracking buildings, I realize that we live in an unstable world. Natural disasters or theft can happen to each and every one of us. I find it best to go though life considering all of my possessions as imperma-nent, placing a greater emphasis on health and inner growth.

We've worked hard and satisfied the economic requirements of hap-piness. We can now harvest the fruits of our labor. It's time for...

SEVEN

Pursuing Pleasure... Intelligently!

Be timid no more.
Life's a sumptuous banquet.
Sample! Explore! Expand!

Planet Earth provides a bounty of sensual and pleasurable potentials, yet we nibble shyly from the edges. We cloister ourselves from new experiences. Our senses are repeatedly re-exposed to the same stimuli. We lose touch with our novelty-seeking drive and slope imperceptibly toward the ordinary, the routine, the unconscious. We wonder why we're not obtaining pleasure and satisfaction from things we used to enjoy. Familiarity turns into routine. One week becomes no different than the week before– or the week after. Eventually, familiarity metamorphoses into a master demanding the same television shows, the same meals, the same vacation spots... *the same everything.*

The pendulum arcs to and fro. Seasons come and go. The borders of comfort zones retreat and bake... like the shores of a drying lake.

It happens to all of us. Familiarity, in very subtle ways, numbs our senses, and saps our initiative. Once aware of this trend, we can take steps to turn the tide. A little effort expands our comfort zone, watering our parched shores. Having made this effort, we realize how easy it is to continue expanding. The first step is the hardest. While in the process of expanding, let's also remind ourselves to *reappreciate* and *love* the familiar, being grateful for everything we already have and are able to do.

Sample! Explore! Expand!

Do you feel stuck in a rut and wish to break free? If so, shatter the eggshell surrounding your senses and step outside. There is so much to experience. Enhance your consciousness by adding variety. Life is a sumptuous banquet and many of its delicacies are free or inexpensive. Why not try something new?

- Camp in a National Park– there are so many to see: Acadia… Zion… Hot Springs… Glacier… *Ah, Wilderness!*

- Create and cook a new recipe: dice, dot, and dredge.

- Seclude to a monastery, convent, temple, or ashram and meditate in *time stands still* silence.

- Write a letter to the editor of a local paper. Express your opinions and feelings. Use gentle words.

- Go on an archeological excavation. What ancestral mysteries lie unseen in subterrestrial soil?

- Attend an acting or improvisation course– doth a Thespian spirit roam restless amid your depths? Voice lessons, perhaps?

- Select an alpine sport. Slide and ski down enchanting Austrian *Sound of Music* snowy slopes.

- Wind, string, or drum in a trio– piccolo, cello, or bongo?

- Climb your state's highest peak. Delawarians, pick a neighboring state's mountain range.

- Grow a garden– plant a pansy, pot some parsley, bud and bloom a lily of the valley. Forget-them-not!

- Bicycle through Vermont's *roads less traveled* kaleidoscopic autumn foliage carrying a pocket volume of Robert Frost poetry.

- Solve a crossword clue– personality trait, four letters, *après* self-

- Enroll in a public speaking course or join *Toastmasters*. People do not know you by what you think, but by what you say and how well you explain yourself.

- Produce a poem and present it to your precious partner.

- Raft the Colorado River; gorge on the greatness of the Grand Canyon.
- Master new steps and tap into terpsichorean talents– country western, minuet, or tip-toe ballet?

Unlimited possibilities await you. List in a journal ideas you come across through conversations, books, and magazines. Try at least one.

As you may have noticed, all the above suggestions involve active involvement. These types of activities absorb our total concentration. They energize us. They seem to provide so much enjoyment and satisfaction that a time distortion occurs. Minutes and hours slow at a snail's pace, or speed like a video tape on fast forward.

Passive types of entertainment– watching television, movies, and going to the theater– are enjoyable, relax us, and sometimes have inspirational qualities. However, they rarely engage our full physical, intellectual, and creative potential, as does active involvement. As a society we over-rely on these passive forms of entertainment at the expense of creative pursuits of pleasure.

The next section discusses how to expand appreciation of sensual pleasures. Take these ideas as stepping stones and propel yourself to your mind's unexplored regions of rapture.

Delight your five senses

Our well-being is very much affected by sensory input. We have a choice over what reaches our mind. Why not enrich our lives with pleasurable stimuli?

Sensual gratification is an art. Senses habituate to frequent exposures of the same stimulus. If you use perfume, you know quite well that within minutes you no longer notice it. Yet others do. The intelligent pursuit of pleasure calls for *variety* and periods of *abstinence* (or *absence*) from a particular exposure. The familiar in our lives becomes more satisfying when we return to it after a period of absence.

Ecstasy may be too strong a word but it closely mirrored my mood when I first boarded *Norwegian Cruise Lines* touring Caribbean islands. My bed was tucked right next to the porthole. Each morning I peeked through the mauve curtains and delighted at the sight of the open ocean or an exotic island. Even now, years later, hearing the name of the isles and ports of call– *Castries on St. Lucia, Megan's Bay on St. Thomas, St. George's on Grenada*– induces turquoise-toned reveries of waving palm fronds, sun-dried driftwood, and footprints-in-sand seashore strolls.

At the end of two years of cruising, although I still enjoyed the lifestyle on the ship, the original wonder had waned. The islands had lost some of their magic. I realized that even 'paradise on earth' can become familiar after a while. I haven't been to the Caribbean for a few years. This period of absence has rekindled a strong urge to revisit.

Here are some specific suggestions on sensual input and stimulation. Add to the following list any others that come to mind.

The art of seeing

When you see beauty in the ordinary and familiar, you have learned the art of seeing. A visual fantasy playland surrounds us, at all times, if only we'd take notice.

Early in the day, as you kick the sheets and blanket away, turn back your head toward your bed. The covers turn into a series of mountain ranges with deep ravines and vast plains. You groggily meander to the bathroom and turn on the shower. Water drops splatter halfway up the tile wall, trickle and dribble, and into each other fall. As you make your way to the kitchen for a warm drink, note the yellow of a banana resting near the sink. Our practical mind filters much of the visual stimuli that surrounds us. My awareness of this visual feast began when I studied photography. I started to notice the endless variety of hues, lighting, textures (rough, smooth), lines (thick, thin, curved, horizontal, vertical), and shapes and shadows, at different times of the day. The more we look, the more we see. Even fumes floating from a factory smokestack can fascinate.

Take an art appreciation course. Expose yourself to new vistas and perspectives. Every time you see a painting in a home, museum, or gallery, you become more aware of its style and beauty. One of my favorite museums is the National Gallery of Art at the Smithsonian Institute in Washington, DC. Its galleries are arranged so that one can walk counterclockwise, from room to room, and see the whole evolution of painting; in periodical succession unfold gothic, renaissance, baroque, romanticism, impressionism, and modern styles.

Travel to lands with unusual geography, culture, and geology. New sights awaken our dormant eyes from their habitual apathy.

There's an inventiveness to seeing. During the summer of 1988, I spent three months working on the *S.S. Independence,* an *American Hawaii Cruise Line* ship. Every evening near sundown, following my afternoon office hours, I strolled up to the deck to stretch out on a lounge chair, sip a strawberry daiquiri, and read. (James Michener's *Hawaii* was one of the books I completed that summer.) Periodically I raised my eyes from the page to watch the floating clouds pass by. Loosening my hold on reality, I envisioned each cloud as a constantly evolving white Rorshach blot. A cloud the shape of a watermelon reformed into a goose, a duck-billed platypus, a seal, and finally, melting scoops of vanilla ice cream. As the sun's yellow-glow disc began its slow descent behind the western horizon, the cumulus forms would often thin and wisp into orange-red streamers.

July eves of balm followed June. The bounds of my imagination loosened and flew... away like a wind-swept balloon.

The art of listening
In order to appreciate the miracle of sound, we first need to value silence. Spend time alone a few minutes a day in a quiet room.

Unwind with nature tapes. Waft with the primeval calls within Okefenokee swamp in Georgia. Ocean-float on a misty sailboat while the mast creaks, a gull shrieks, and the hull is splashed by salt-spray.

Saunter on wet sand at twilight...breathe in unison with the ocean... drift into an altered state...and let the ageless waves tell a timeless tale.

Attend poetry readings, offer no resistance, and ride on the poet's subliminal words to realms of unreal worlds.

We rarely have the opportunity to escape the clamor of cars, airplanes, machinery, television, and other myriad sounds in our lives. In September 1986, I took a ten day canoe trip sponsored by the *American Youth Hostel Organization*. We explored the Boundary Waters of northern Minnesota, a region of countless, crystal-pure lakes. Twelve of us were on the trip, each from a different state. As the journey progressed, a great camaraderie blossomed. We bonded with each other. Wilderness has a tendency to dissolve ego boundaries. Every day, having paddled hour upon hour, enduring the strenuous portaging of the canoes and equipment between lakes, we set up camp, cooked dinner, and sat around a fire. After a few songs, a conundrum or two, and a round of charades, each person, one by one, would retire to his or her tent. Charles, from Boston, and I would remain. We seemed to be the only two who truly appreciated the night silence of the northern woods. Yet, it was not a complete silence. As the stone-circled, snapping fire logs shrank to cinders, dwindling into ever-dimming embers, and powdering into ash, previously subdued sounds emerged. Charles and I sat on a blanket on the banks of the dark lake contoured by birches, fir, and spruce. Slowly and deeply we inhaled the cool night air of the unspoiled northern woods. Our eyes were closed; no words were spoken. There was no need to speak. Silence connected us. Our ears fine-tuned to nature's harmony. *Listen…*

> *to the surround sound peace:*
> *the owl, and the echo*
> *hoot-hooting at habitual intervals…*
> *the soft chatter of chilled crickets*
> *oscillating in coherent heaves…*
> *an occasional loon's haunting cry*
> *eerily screeching through blackness…*
> *and a rare, plaintive wail, of a far…*
> *far distant wolf.*
> *All this orchestrated*
> *with the barely audible*
> *whisper of a breeze*
> *sweeping across*
> *the still lake.*

Good scents

Smells influence us more than we think. They trigger memories. Real estate agents are aware that the odor of freshly baked bread sells houses. Used car salesmen enhance old jalopies with the scent of turtle wax.

Play a game with friends using a box of condiments, herbs, and spices. Close your eyes and try to guess as many as possible.

Identify and remember the scents of popular perfumes and colognes. Can you identify the different ones flattering your friends, co-workers, spouse, or lover?

Visit an arboretum. Write in a journal the names of plants and flowers that have a scent. Hold someone's hand, drop your eyelids blind, walk through a path of flora, and identify new bouquets.

Indulge in aromatherapy where squadrons of aromatic, aerosol molecules pleasantly bombard your keen, olfactory sense– each sortie soaring from the bath water floods overjoyed nasal receptors.

On your way to work or school each morning, do you notice the lone lily, sweet jasmine, or radiant rose that you pass?

The lonely flower
flushes her alluring fragrance
(as your footsteps approach)
beckoning for attention;
"smell my fragrance," she blushes...
"connect with me."

Stimulating skin sensation

Give and receive a massage by someone dear to you– a great way to relax at the close of a work week. Caress the soft fur of a pet. Give back the unconditional love. Hug friends and family who are receptive; it's a wonderful way to connect. Feel a session of foot reflexology– have someone's fingers walk on your heel. Our feet can give us more pleasure than we give them credit.

Take warm baths before going to bed. Let your cares flutter into the horizon on the wings of a soaring seagull. The warmth releases serotonin, a neurotransmitter associated with sleep and relaxation. The result is more restful slumber.

Sweat in a Jacuzzi or sauna. Unwind coiled muscles. Let tension dissipate and disperse in the moist heat.

In June of 1989, I experienced the thrill of a week long river rafting trip down the Rogue river in Oregon. On the fourth night of the trip the leader of our group decided to give us a treat. None of us had washed for days and felt sticky and dirty. He placed long branches in the shape of a tepee, and enveloped it with a large tarpaulin sheet. This was an improvised sweat lodge. Drops of water were trickled on smooth, round, fire-heated rocks. The tepee became unbearably hot from the steam and we started to sweat profusely. A brave soul suggested we take a dip into the river. There were no objections. We hurried out of the tepee. Reflecting moonlight, our naked bodies dove into the rushing waters. We laughed and howled from dermal sensory overload. This process of *running into the tepee–* sweat– *running into the river–* freeze– repeated several times. I had the perception that every skin pore on my body opened and closed, discharging impurities. I never felt cleaner in my life. That night, I slipped into my sleeping bag in the cloudless open air… embraced by the full canopy of heavenly stars. I slept… a so sweet sleep… at one with the river and the woods.

Tickle your taste buds

Sample an array of ethnic restaurants– Peruvian, Moroccan, Indonesian, Grecian. Make a list in a journal of the various exotic foods that you have relished. How's your soup consciousness? Have you spooned gazpacho, avgolemono, dashi, or minestrone?

Remember to eat in a slow manner when invited for homemade dinner. Acknowledge the care it took to cook. A compliment be sure to deal, that is, if you like the meal.

Experiment with a different condiment. Fashion a fresh dish, astonish yourself with the luscious concoction, and savor the lip-licking flavor.

Why not imbibe from a glass at a wine tasting class?

Fast on occasion and reappreciate the taste of food. Abstain from a favorite dish to the point where you actually crave it. Our sense of taste is not unlike the other senses in its disposition to fatigue by overexposure. During my last year of medical school I tried an experiment on myself by not eating anything sweet or sugary for a month. Three weeks into the experiment, as I was studying in the library, hunger pangs disturbed my concentration. The only source of food was a vending machine selling sodas and orange juice. Two quarters in the slot dropped a four ounce carton of juice. I opened the carton, took a gulp, and was soon nauseated. I looked at the carton. It actually said 'orangeade.' It was thickened with added sugar. The three week absence from sugar made my tongue virgin to sweetness... to the verge of vomiting. Before the experiment, I would have easily tolerated sugared drinks. I pondered centuries past when sweeteners were such precious products, the dropping of a honey dollop in morning porridge must have been rapturously prized. In these modern times of cornucopic abundance our taste buds have been numbed beyond boredom.

The intent of this chapter is to encourage you to expand your horizons. The more variety imprinted in the brain, the richer the memory bank and the fuller life will feel. When you reflect upon the year that just passed, what comes to mind? Take a moment and list a few meaningful events from the past year. Events most often remembered are those that are unusual and/or stimulating. Vacations, special encounters with family or loved ones, significant events at work or school, public speaking, and other performances are all unforgettable.

The rest of this chapter focuses on the exciting themes of travel, music, movies, and nature.

Expanding comfort zones

Travel is intensified living. It shakes, slaps, and douses a pail of ice water on our routine-slothed senses, stimulating and rousing our entire being to an enhanced awareness. Furthermore, it shows us multiple perspectives, encouraging us to extend beyond the *cocoonish* view of our world.

Make it a point in your lifetime to visit the well-known cities and important historical and archeological sites such as New York, Washington DC, London, Paris, Rome, Venice, Vienna, the Great Pyramids, Machu Pichu, the Parthenon, Taj Mahal, the Great Wall of

China, and Kyoto, Japan. Alternate vacations between cities and rural areas, hot and cold regions, rainy and dry, desert and ocean. "To appreciate heaven well," wrote William Carelton (1845-1912), the American Poet, "Tis good for a man to have fifteen minutes of hell." Contrast improves appreciation.

Vacations provide novel and exciting challenges that allow your mind to drift to new shores. It may take as long as three to four days to unwind on a vacation and begin to fully notice and participate in one's new environment. Getting away from it all brings new outlooks and solutions to old problems.

Give yourself a break. If you have a type A personality, park it in the garage while you're sauntering through distant lands. School and office work are also best left behind. Reading newspapers and keeping up with the news on vacation may interfere with your mind's attempt to escape the familiar, defeating the purpose of a holiday.

Travel off-season when crowds, long lines, and inflated prices are at a minimum. The enjoyment of a particular city or country varies significantly at different times of the year. "Visit Paris in August?" you ask. *Ooh la la! Not on your Notre Dame!* Only if you care to see Mona Lisa at the Louvre within the length of a football field and lit up by hundreds of flashbulbs.

Covering too much territory may dilute your experience. Take advantage and enjoy wherever you are and feel the pulse of the region before moving on. It's physically and mentally exhausting to try to visit multiple countries or cities in a short period of time.

If you have a choice between a long vacation on a tight budget or a shorter one on a looser budget, choose the latter to avoid constant financial worry. Sometimes trying to save a few dollars backfires. Eating at an inexpensive and unsanitary restaurant or from a street vendor in a foreign country may result in a case of diarrhea or viral hepatitis. A fourth class ticket during a long train ride will leave you exhausted if sardined in a congested compartment. Compare that to a relaxing, enjoyable ride in first or second class.

When choosing to take a book along on a trip, I try to pick an author from the region I'm visiting. For example, on my trip to Cornwall, England, I read *Rebecca* by Daphne Du Maurier. It added another dimension to my appreciation of the region.

Read about the history of the country in order to appreciate the archeological sites and points of interest. Meet the locals whether you are in Krakow, Karachi, or Katmandu. Many interesting, lesser known points of interest can be discovered by striking up conversations with locals. Some of my best travel memories are those that involved human interaction and connection.

When we are in another culture, the proper attitude is one of respect. Accept the citizens as they are. After all, we are guests. Upon returning from vacation, give yourself at least a day or two of winding down and solidifying cherished memories before diving back into work.

Music– opium for the ears

Overexposure to music is something we rarely consider. In the morning, many of us wake to the radio, and are thereafter barraged by music in the car, at work, in shopping malls, elevators, and waiting rooms.

A few years ago, I noticed that my appreciation for music had diminished. Perhaps my radio was on too much at home. I vividly remember hearing a song by Phil Collins in a Jackson, Wyoming, alpine clothing store after a week long camping trip in the Grand Tetons. It sounded so good! I found myself attentively frozen by the speaker, mesmerized by the melody. I had heard the same song many times previously, but it never had made an impression on me. At that point I realized how overexposure to music had diminished my enjoyment. The week long stillness in the mountains had cleared my head and readjusted my musical appreciation threshold. I imagined the Middle Ages where peasants tortuously toiled in fields from dismal dawn to dim dusk, season after season. Only on singular occasions would they have the opportunity to cross the imposing arched gates of a cathedral, humbly rest on a pew, and revel in the astonishing polyphony of Gregorian chanting or the resounding vocals of a choir. I pictured their smiles of delight as each quivering note reverberated off buttressed walls and lofty gothic vaults, echoing into their acoustically famished ears. These chants must have sounded heavenly. Along a similar line, how exciting it must have been to attend an annual village fair and be entertained by visiting troubadours.

A cherished piece of music loses its novelty when repeatedly played. One of my favorite classical symphonies is Beethoven's Fifth. It an unforgettable masterpiece; I never want to tire of it. I listen to it only once a year, on New Year's day. The act of anticipation, that is, looking forward to a pleasurable experience– not only in music, but in everything else– is part of the overall gratification. Each time I hear this forty minute symphony it reaffirms my love of Beethoven's creative genius. Have you had favorite songs or CDs lose their appeal after repeated exposures? Store them away for a few months and listen to them on special occasions. All our senses fatigue if not introduced to variety or periods of abstinence. Sometimes I have cried in joy while listening to a CD that I haven't heard for a while. In music appreciation– as with other forms of sensual gratification– sometimes 'less is more.'

When listening to a song you've heard before, single out one instrument or vocal and focus your attention on it.

Expand your musical horizon by taking a music appreciation course at a local college. Learn the history of music from medieval to renaissance, baroque, classical, romantic, modern, gospel, blues, jazz, folk, rock, country, new age, rap, and ambient. Taking a course in classical music served to enhance my enjoyment.

Ask your friends about their favorite CDs. Listen to music from a variety of styles, cultures, and countries. We are fortunate to live in an era where crystal clear, quality recorded music from every corner of the globe is readily available.

Movies and entertainment– mind adventure without leaving town

If you have the time and the interest, rent the *Academy Award* winning best films chronologically from 1927 to the present. The first winner was *Wings*. The following year, the winner was *Broadway Melody*. Some of these early movies are not that sophisticated by today's standards, but it's fascinating to see how movies have transformed over the last few decades and how they reflect changing times. You can find a list of these films in the *World Almanac* available in bookstores. Buy a movie guide and each time you see a film write the month and the year next to the title. As with anything else, watching movies too frequently takes away the magic. This also holds true for television. The longer we watch the less likely we are to enjoy. Furthermore, studies show that those who watch long hours tend to lose personal motivation. They become less happy since they begin to compare their humdrum life to *live life to the fullest* characters on television and the silver screen. Humans have a tendency to base their satisfaction in life on how everyone else is doing. If others are seen to be better off, expectations are raised of what one's own life should be. When these expectations are not met disappointment is certain to follow. TV viewing also increases the desire for material objects, obviously due to the endless fusillade of cleverly-crafted ads.

For additional entertainment, try opera, ballet, local theater groups, or improvisation and comedy clubs. Why not create your own home movies?

Nature– a teacher, a friend, a boundless beauty

Nature reveals her majesty and subtle mysteries to those who take the time to unwind, slow down to her leisurely pace, and embrace her endless wonders with an open heart.

Most of us rarely take the time to notice the elegant symmetry that surrounds us. Take a walk outside and look around you. Look around and imagine seeing it for the first time– like a child. See the perfection in a slender spear of grass. Raise your head and stare in wonder at the ephemeral clouds floating gracefully. "Will the clouds ever be arranged *just so* again?" asks my dear friend Matthew as we sit on a straw-colored hill watching clouds form on Monterey Bay.

Do you take a look at the tree you walk by every day? "I think that I shall never see, a poem lovely as a tree," wrote Joyce Kilmer (1886-1918), the American poet.

It is true,
the lovely pine tree,
whose terminal bough touches
the wooden railing of my third-floor balcony
stands firm– content with its plot of land.
Green needles and brown boughs
sparkle in the setting sun.
This pine tree is my silent neighbor–
silent until its wispy needles
whistle and rustle
awakened by evening waves
of ocean-breath.

Learning the names of the birds, trees, and flowers indigenous to our environment influences our awareness. "To people uninstructed in natural history," wrote Thomas Huxley (1825-95), the English scientist and humanist, "Their country or seaside stroll is a walk through a gallery filled with wonderful works of art, nine-tenths of which have their faces turned to the wall." Field trips with the *Sierra Club, Audubon Society,* and other environmental organizations are helpful in learning more about our 'nature gallery.' These groups also present the opportunity to meet and build friendships with wonderful people.

Solitude has the power to heal. It is not a luxury, but a necessity. Leave civilization at least once a year. Even if it's only for a few days, the psychic rest and relaxation are healing. Distance yourself from cars, television, and other reminders of our modern, urban pace. Free from distractions, get in touch with your inner self. Awaken at morning's muted, early light in the midst of a dew-moist meadow. The stillness calms city-strained nerves. Recline on a rock by a mountain creek and let the soothing current of the water answer your meditative thoughts. Allow your cares and concerns to float downstream on the backs of golden autumn leaves.

Backpacking and camping make us feel the absence of our daily amenities. As a consequence, we learn to revalue our home comforts (softer beds, toilets, running water, variety of foods, and hot showers).

Nature is art. We can enhance our appreciation of her wonders even more by taking time to study landscapes in their infinite varieties. Photograph, draw, paint, or write poetry inspired by a particularly appealing scene. Take time to bird watch, look for animal tracks, search and identify wild flowers, notice the shapes of leaves and geological features. "What is life?" asked Crowfoot, (1821-1890), the Blackfoot warrior and orator. "It is the flash of a firefly in the night. It is the breath of a buffalo in the winter time. It is the little shadow which runs across the grass and loses itself in the sunset."

A few months before this book was published, I took a trip up the northern coast of California. The experience of one special evening on a beach prompted me to compose the following poem:

Ivory-hued pebbles on little feet
moan, roar, retreat.
Wild waves crash and pebbles meet
moan, roar, repeat.
Mammoth Sea Lion lumbering dark
groans a heavy sigh on rocky isle rock
arches his neck, to growl and bark
while his whiskers by moonlight spark.

Wild waves crash and pebbles meet
retreat, repeat, retreat.
Desolate shadows of Cypress Tree display
crags crashed
by savage sea and spray.

The Sea Lion dives into the darkly deep sapphire sea.

Our experience of nature is enhanced whenever we take the time to think about it and attentively focus on its myriad aspects. Writing the above poem took concentration, and the very act itself heightened my awareness. If you've never written poetry, do make an attempt. Even if the poem does not sound great to you, the time spent in observation and thinking provides a warm glow inside and makes a deeper imprint of the scene on memory.

Throughout my travels I have noticed a significant difference in my appreciation of nature's beauty depending on whether the travel was motorized or self-propelled. Whenever I have traveled by car or bus, each stop at a scenic point did not induce the same awe or wonder as did reaching a scenic point by bicycle or foot (hiking or backpacking). Physical exertion intensifies one's appreciation of scenery. The exertion makes one feel part of nature, rather than being a spectator. The endorphin release through exertion induces a wonderful mix of energy and calmness.

When was the last time you *really saw* a sunrise or a sunset?

Oh yes, before I forget, let us not overlook life's simple daily pleasures: drying the dishes, dialing the phone, dusting the bookcase, darning the socks…

Physical and mental health are the bedrock from which we soar and frolic in our mind's uncharted pleasure paradise, just as it is easier to scale a mountain peak from a well-established base camp. So

> slip on your aerobic shoes
> stoop and stretch your sinews
> pop an antioxidant pill
> fill a juice mug to the sill
> (carrots, kale and dill?)
> *sip, sip,* and with lip moist
> hoist your mug and toast to…

EIGHT

Nurturing Physical & Mental Health

Mind/brain and body are one.

During my years of medical practice I have treated countless individuals who wished they had taken better care of their bodies in their youth. Sometimes it takes a significant jolt, such as a heart attack, to rouse a person from the slumbering neglect of their health.

Our physical body should be treated with the utmost respect and care. It is more important than all our material possessions including our car, home, and jewelry.

A healthy body is essential to a healthy and happy mind. A disturbance of one eventually affects the other. Let us nurture our health before irreversible damage occurs. A simple cold can make us feel miserable; imagine the impact a serious disease can have on our sense of well-being. Many people ignore their health. Instead, they spend hours polishing their car and cleaning their home. Material possessions are replaceable; we only have one body.

Being healthy is *not* merely the absence of disease. Rather, It means having endless energy, the drive to be active, to create, to pursue goals, and to live every moment to the fullest. When physically and mentally healthy we rarely suffer from colds, aches, stiffness, anxiety, or listlessness. A strong immune system protects us from the constant exposure to unfriendly germs. The sense of well-being accompanying health and vigor strongly influences our level of happiness, modifying the way we experience the world. Daily troubles or problems seem easier to solve. Being truly healthy gives us the capacity to tackle and overcome any obstacle. A natural high pervades us as we go on with our daily routine.

We become lighter on our feet, walk with a bounce, and radiate an irresistible presence.

I once knew a pulmonary specialist in Philadelphia who treated patients suffering from lung cancer, emphysema, and other chronic lung diseases. Some of these patients had reduced lung capacities and would struggle through his office door gasping for breath at every step. Some even wore nasal cannulas, with tubing connected to oxygen canisters, that they trailed along. It is difficult to believe that this lung specialist was a *two pack a day smoker.* I learned a valuable lesson by observing him: knowledge of facts does not necessarily translate into their implementation.

This chapter discusses nutrition, exercise, sleep, relaxation, mental health, and common sense guidelines to a healthy life. Consult your physician before making any significant changes.

Nutrition

Proper nutrition is crucial to a healthy body and mind, and thus, *happiness.* There are countless substances in the foods and drinks we consume that can directly or indirectly affect our neurotransmitters.

No two physicians or nutritionists will agree on all details of dietary recommendations. My guidelines are all based on the latest scientific research. I have made every effort to be as accurate as possible. Nutritional investigations are ongoing and further studies will inevitably elucidate many of our present uncertainties, and possibly contradict some earlier studies. Remember, the wonderful aspect of science is that it has the ability to correct itself as new information materializes.

Foods are basically composed of three major nutrients and two categories of minor nutrients. They also contain indigestible material called fiber (or roughage) which is usually found as part of the complex carbohydrates. The major nutrients are carbohydrates, proteins, and fats.

Carbohydrates should ideally provide 60-80% of one's caloric intake. They are subdivided into *complex* and *simple. Complex carbohydrates* are found in grains, starches, vegetables, and legumes. (Legumes also contain a good amount of protein.) Complex sources are much healthier than simple carbohydrates. *Simple carbohydrates* are the sugars such as fructose (from fruits), glucose (fruits, honey), and sucrose (made from sugar cane, it consists of glucose and fructose).

Protein is found in meat, fish, fowl, and dairy. Most protein foods also contain fat. Legumes have a high protein content but little fat. Ten to twenty percent of one's diet should be composed of protein. Many people believe the myth that protein generates strength and that the best source of protein is meat. Strength comes through exercise, and a good source of energy for exercise comes from complex carbohydrates.

Fats are composed of molecules called *fatty acids* that are categorized as *saturated, monounsaturated,* and *polyunsaturated. Saturated fats* are found in animal fat, lard, suet, cream, cheese, and meat. Coconut and palm kernel oils are also mostly saturated. *Monounsaturated fats* are found in some vegetable oils such as olive (use extra virgin), canola (rapeseed), and many nuts. *Polyunsaturated fats* are found in most vegetable oils. There are some polyunsaturated fatty acids that the body is unable to make. They are called essential fatty acids (EFA's), and need to be supplied through diet. Alpha-linolenic acid (ALA) is available through flax, hemp seed, soybean, walnut, and dark green leafy vegetables. Flax seed is an excellent source. ALA is used to make Eicosapentanoic acid (EPA), necessary in the manufacture of important chemicals in our body called prostaglandins, series 3. Linoleic acid is also essential. It is found mostly in safflower, sunflower, corn, hemp seed, soybean, evening primrose, and wheat germ.

You may notice some food labels list 'hydrogenated oils.' This means that during the cooking process, hydrogen atoms were added to the oils to make them more solid, and saturated. During the manufacturing of margarine and vegetable shortening, hydrogenation changes the shape of these fats creating artificial forms called *trans fatty acids.* Higher consumption of these fats is associated with an increased incidence of heart disease. Danish pastry, doughnuts, and french fries are especially high in trans fatty acids. Fat should comprise less than 20% of daily calories since a high fat diet increases the risk of heart disease and cancer. Learning and memory are enhanced in rats fed a low fat diet. On the average, Americans consume 35-40% of their calories from fat.

The minor nutrients include vitamins and minerals. Vitamins include A, B complex, C, D, E, and K. Beta-carotene, found in fruits and vegetables, is a precursor to vitamin A. The B complex includes thiamin (B1), riboflavin (B2), niacin, pantothenic acid, pyridoxine (B6), para-aminobenzoic acid, biotin, folic acid, and cyanocobalamin (B12).

Minerals include calcium, chromium, copper, iodine, iron, magnesium, manganese, molybdenum, phosphorus, potassium, selenium, and zinc.

Nutritional investigations indicate that a diet low in fat, calories, and animal protein, and high in fiber, legumes, cereals, fruits, vegetables, and antioxidant vitamins prolongs life. This diet reduces the risk of infection, cardiovascular disease (heart attack, hypertension, and stroke), cancer, diabetes, and other chronic illnesses. The risk for some adult neurological diseases, such as stroke, Alzheimer's, and Parkinson's, is also likely to be reduced. The evidence is based on metabolic, animal, and epidemiological studies.

A study published in the December 16, 1993, *Journal of the American Medical Association* indicates that lifespan can be prolonged by eating less and staying thin. Harvard University alumni were followed from 1962 to 1988. Lowest mortality was among men weighing 20% below the US average for men of comparable age and height. Studies in laboratory animals repeatedly indicate the correlation between eating less and living longer. In one study three groups of rats were used: the first group was fed normally, the second group was overfed, and the third group was underfed. The type of food remained consistent in all groups. The underfed rats lived longer, had fewer cancers, and had a decreased incidence of heart disease. The restricted diet also slowed down the brain's aging process. The leaner rats had more energy, better memory and learning ability, and were more active, while the overfed rats were sluggish and lazy. The benefits of caloric restriction were realized even with rats that began the diet after middle age.

A possible explanation: compare the body to a car. A car consumes gas for energy while the body consumes food. The burning of gas produces byproducts which are discarded through the exhaust system. In the body the byproducts of metabolism are detoxified within the cells.

They are then excreted through the intestinal and urinary systems. The byproducts of metabolism increase proportionally to the amount of food consumed and metabolized. An overabundance of toxins overburdens the cells' ability to neutralize them. Some of these toxic metabolites are called free radicals (superoxide, hydrogen peroxide, hydroxyl) and accumulate within the cells resulting in microscopic damage to the cell wall, DNA, and mitochondria. Free radicals are also thought to cause damage to neurons in the brain, causing premature senility. Smoking is known to produce free radicals.

One theory of aging is that this slow damage decreases the ability of cells to function properly, causing disease and premature death. This damage is partly due to the process of oxidation– the process that causes metal to rust and butter to turn rancid. Fats and oils (especially polyunsaturated) are more likely to produce free radicals than carbohydrates and proteins. Antioxidant vitamins and nutrients help mop up these free radicals, protecting the cell from damage.

Cell death is also regulated by genetic programming. A cell undergoes a predetermined number of divisions before it dies. Cancer cells lose part of the genetic factor that causes cells to stop dividing. This is why cancer cells continually divide and multiply; they are practically immortal. In the future scientists may identify this genetically programmed factor and find ways to prolong lifespan even more.

Lightening the load on bathroom scales

It's not easy for some individuals to stay thin– they may have a genetic predisposition for obesity. Nevertheless there are some rational steps that can be taken, and some thoughts to keep in mind:

> Love yourself no matter how much you weigh. Food is your friend, not your foe. Any change in dietary habits should be done gradually to enable the body to adjust itself metabolically. Losing weight is best done for the purposes of improved health and well-being rather than for social purposes or vanity. Drastic diets are not best for permanent weight loss. A steady loss of a pound or two a month is quite satisfactory.

If a complete approach is not taken, and the essentials covered in other chapters of this book are not fulfilled, losing weight will be a *Sisyphus-like* labor. (In Greek mythology, Sisyphus was a king who offended Zeus. As punishment, he was forced to roll an enormous boulder to the top of a steep hill. Every time the boulder neared the top, it would roll back down, and Sisyphus had to start all over again.) A complete approach helps prevent this seesaw-like process. Eating may be one of the few daily pleasures available to those who are going through difficult periods in their lives. I have noticed myself raiding the refrigerator during periods of restlessness and boredom. When my time is filled with purpose and happiness, eating takes a secondary role. During the creation of this book I would often come home at 6 pm. Instead of eating dinner I would immediately sit at my computer and start writing, completely engrossed and unaware of the passing of hours. Soon the clock showed 2 or 3 am and I had forgotten to eat. At one point I had lost fifteen pounds, although I was already thin. Find interests and activities that give you more sustained mood elevation than eating.

Self-monitoring is at the core of behavioral weight loss programs. Those who keep food records achieve weight loss goals more easily. Caloric intake is spontaneously reduced when daily records are kept. Carry a small, hand-sized journal in your pocket or purse. Notice environmental cues that trigger your eating and modify your reaction. Set aside specific times and places to eat. Give yourself prizes for achieving exercise and weight loss goals. Taste and enjoy each small morsel to its fullest before swallowing. There is no need to force yourself to finish a plate; the leftovers can be saved for another meal. If you binge occasionally, don't feel guilty. If your diet is normally good and you have an occasional craving for a particularly unhealthy food, go ahead and splurge without feeling guilty. If you have a strong desire to eat an unhealthy food regularly, eat small portions. Calories from carbohydrates are less fattening than calories from fat since a quarter of the calories from carbohydrates burn as they are being converted into body fat.

Exercise is essential to healthy weight loss; it speeds metabolism, increases the rate at which calories are burned, and tones muscles. These positive benefits continue hours beyond the period of activity. The importance of physical activity cannot be overemphasized.

Vitamins, minerals, and nutrients
The medical establishment has been cautious about recommending nutrient supplements to the public since studies have shown conflicting results. In my view, however, the overall evidence is in favor of supplementation with at least some antioxidant nutrients. They help neutralize free radicals and are likely to reduce the rates of heart disease, cancer, emphysema, infection, and cataracts. Supplementation could prolong life span and reduce the incidence of many illnesses.

Vitamin C reduces the risk of cancer, specifically esophagus, larynx, oral cavity, pancreas, and probably stomach and cervical. Regular ingestion lessens the severity and length of a cold, helps with bronchitis and other lung infections, and protects against heart disease. At the earliest onset of a cold, take 5 grams or more (1 gram equals 1000 mg). This will sometimes help prevent it. (Zinc lozenges may also help prevent worsening of a cold.) Good dietary sources of vitamin C are citrus fruits such as oranges and grapefruit, and tropical fruits such as mangoes, guavas, and kiwi. Vegetable sources include broccoli, cauliflower, and peppers. I take additional supplements of 250 to 1000 mg. After taking chewable vitamin C, rinse your mouth with water or brush your teeth as the sugar and acid in these supplements can cause cavities.

Vitamin E protects against gastrointestinal, lung, and bladder cancers. This vitamin reduces the risk of heart disease and angina (chest pain). Rats fed supplemental vitamin E had less accumulation of *lipofuscin* (the age pigment which indicates neuronal damage) in their brain. Good dietary sources are limited. It is not possible to obtain enough vitamin E from foods for maximal antioxidant protection. Most days I take 100 to 400 units.

In addition to the above antioxidants, I frequently take a B complex that includes thiamin 10 mg, riboflavin 10 mg, pyridoxine 10 mg, niacinamide 100 mg, pantothenic acid 50 mg, biotin 300 mcg, folic acid 400 mcg, cobalamin 20 mcg, and para-aminobenzoic acid 10 mg. My multimineral supplement includes calcium 500 mg, chromium 30 mcg, copper 1 mg, magnesium 200 mg, manganese 5 mg, molybdenum 20 mcg, selenium 100 mcg, and zinc 15 mg.

No one can accurately tell you how much, if any, of the above supplements you need. You have a unique chemistry. Because optimum doses have not been determined, how much to take remains a personal decision. Although not all the nutrients necessary for optimum health and longevity have been thoroughly studied, the following are a few that show great promise.

Carotenoids, bright red and yellow pigments occurring in plants, are introduced into humans through vegetables and fruits. So far, 600 carotenoids have been identified; fifty of these are thought to have health-promoting benefits, protecting us from cancer and heart disease. Good dietary sources include carrots, squash, sweet potatoes, green leafy vegetables, mangoes, cantaloupes, and apricots. A glass of carrot juice contains 50,000-100,000 units of beta-carotene. Tomatoes, red peppers, and red grapefruit have *lycopene* which is twice as effective as beta-carotene at scavenging singlet oxygen. Spinach has *zeazanthin*. Oranges are high in *canthaxanthin,* a more effective antioxidant of peroxyl radicals (H-O-O) than beta-carotene. Green vegetables including broccoli, brussels sprouts, cabbage, and kale have carotenes called *lutein* and *epoxy* and may reduce cancer risk. Beta-carotene is the best studied carotenoid, but in the future, others may be found to be as or more beneficial. The doses of carotenoids necessary for optimum health have not yet been established. *Carotenemia* is the name for the orange hue to palms and soles due to consuming a lot of carotenes–it's harmless. There is no reason to take beta-carotene supplements if your diet includes a wide range of fruits and vegetables.

Flavonoids are other plant chemicals present in fruits, vegetables, herbs, cereals, tea, and wine. The average Western diet contains approximately 1 gram a day. Thousands of different flavonoids have been identified. *Apigenin, catechin, hesperidin, kaempferol, naringenin, quercetin, rutin,* and *tangeretin* are some examples. Quercetin is thought to be the best flavonoid antioxidant found thus far. Flavonoids act as antioxidants, reduce inflammation, thin the blood, protect against heart disease, fight bacteria, and inhibit tumor growth. Protection against histamine release in allergies has also been noted. A study in Holland found a reduced rate of heart attacks in those who had a high flavonoid intake. Eight ounces a day of cranberry juice has been found to decrease the frequency of urinary tract infections in women. Could it be partly due to its quercetin content? Quercetin is found in high concentrations in strawberries, other berries, apricots, and cherries. A pound of strawberries contains 150 mg of quercetin. Naringenin is found in grapefruit juice. Catechin is found in green tea.

In addition to carotenoids and flavonoids, hundreds of other health-promoting substances are found in plants. Many of these plant chemicals *(phytochemicals)* protect against cancer and improve immunity. *Limonene* is found in citrus fruits. Garlic, onions, leeks, and chives have *allyl sulfides.* Broccoli contains *dithiolthiones.* Grapes have *ellagic acid.* Soybeans and dried beans have *protease inhibitors, phytosterols,* and *saponins.* Cruciferous vegetables (bok choy, cabbage, cauliflower, turnips) contain *indoles* and *isothiocyanates.* I believe that consuming a wide variety of grains, legumes, vegetables, and fruits promotes health more than popping megadoses of vitamins.

Nutritional research is proceeding at a fast pace. Other nutrients that show promise include *Ubiquinone-10* (coenzyme Q-10 or CoQ-10), *Acetyl-l-carnitine* (ALCAR), *dimethylaminoethanol* (DMAE), *phosphotidylserine*, *N-acetyl-l-cysteine* (NAC), *ginkgo biloba, ginseng, catalase, glutathione,* and *superoxide dismutase.* Over the next few years we'll learn much more about these and other nutrients, and their combinations.

Potpourri suggestions

The inner lining of our intestinal tract is inhabited by trillions of bacteria comprising hundreds of varieties. Some of these bacteria are beneficial, others produce toxins that are absorbed into the bloodstream causing unhealthy effects. In order to minimize the colonization of these unfriendly germs, we can provide more of the beneficial bacteria through foods such as low or non-fat yogurt (make sure it says "active cultures added" on the label) or take supplements such as *Lactobacillus* and

Bifidobacteria (available in health food stores). These beneficial bacteria occupy the lining of the mouth, pharynx, and the rest of the gastrointestinal system making it less likely for other harmful bacteria, fungi, or viruses to get a foothold. This reduces the frequency of colds, vaginal infections *(yeast/ candidiasis),* and possibly urinary and diarrheal illnesses. Antibiotics destroy many bacteria in the intestines. These supplements are especially useful after a course of antibiotic treatment. Eating complex carbohydrates promotes the growth of bifidobacteria. Keep these supplements refrigerated.

If you're over thirty, taking a children's aspirin (about 80 mg) two to three times a week is of benefit (unless you suffer from a bleeding disorder). Aspirin prevents platelets from sticking together and forming clots, thus improving the flow of blood through the circulatory system. It minimizes the clots that attach inside blood vessels causing strokes and heart attacks. Preliminary reports indicate that colon cancer rates are lower in those who take aspirin supplements. Too much aspirin is counterproductive because it can cause stomach ulcers and kidney injury.

Fiber in the form of psyllium powder (sold in supermarkets under many brand names) provides additional roughage. The powder is mixed in a glass of water or other beverage. I take a teaspoon once a day with a meal. Psyllium reduces the risk for colon cancer and lowers cholesterol levels. Routine use increases stool bulk and regulates the intestinal tract. A good bowel movement can surprisingly elevate one's mood.

When food shopping, buy a vegetable, fruit, grain or legume that you have never tried before. There is an enormous variety of foods from around the world in the supermarkets. Most of us do not take advantage of this bounty. When was the last time you ate *kumquats, chicory, spaghetti squash,* or *cous-cous?*

Purchase snacks such as apples, bananas, fat-free cookies, fig bars, unbuttered air-popped popcorn, and carrot sticks. Next time you're at home with the munchies, reach for a healthy snack.

Vegetable juices are a great alternative to sodas or sugared drinks. Experiment by juicing different vegetables mixed with carrot juice– such as kale, parsley, beets, cucumber, spinach, etc. Wash all fruits and vegetables to reduce pesticide remnants.

Some of us forget to drink enough fluids throughout the day. I try to drink at least four glasses. Drinking a large glass or two of water soon after awakening in the morning stimulates peristalsis of the intestines and evacuation of the bowels. The risk of kidney stones can be decreased by drinking more fluids. (A high calcium diet, or calcium supplements, surprisingly also reduces the risk for kidney stones.)

Heavy coffee drinkers slightly increase their risk of heart disease. Those who ingest more than four cups of coffee a day experience anxiety and are more likely to interpret minor events as stressful. Coffee is a diuretic that flushes out minerals such as calcium and magnesium. This urinary loss continues three hours or more after drinking. The kidneys never adapt to caffeine and keep leaching out these minerals, day after day. Heavy drinkers, especially women, are more likely to develop osteoporosis (thinning of the bones). This thinning can be significantly reduced by calcium supplements and exercising.

Cholesterol levels can be lowered by snacking multiple times a day rather than eating three large meals. A clove of garlic a day also lowers cholesterol levels (and frequency of social dates). When cooking a meal, use less sugar and fat than asked for in the recipe. Substitute lemon juice or broth for seasoning instead of butter, and replace cream and whole milk with skim or low fat milk. Steam, broil, bake, boil, or microwave instead of frying in oil. Salt restriction is only necessary for individuals who are hypertensive. I have a staple meal that I prepare by boiling lentils, wild rice, and barley for half an hour. Towards the end of the cooking, chopped scallions, garlic, tofu pieces, various condiments, and frozen vegetables can be added, along with a little bit of polyunsaturated oil.

Most of us are normally too rushed when we eat. Take the time to savor every bite. We are lucky that we live in a land of abundance. All types of food from around the world are available at every season. Let's appreciate this fortune. Chew slowly with love and gratefulness remembering Khalil Gibran's soulful words, "When you crush an apple with your teeth, say to it in your heart, your seeds shall live in my body… and your fragrance shall be my breath."

The ideal diet

Modern nutritional research has given us a great deal of information on the benefits and harms of different foods. Why not take advantage of this information to become more energetic and live longer? In a nutshell, *the ideal diet includes a variety of grains, legumes, fruits, starches, and vegetables.*

Eat to your delight

Attempt to make the following foods at least two thirds of your total food intake. Eat as much as you want since they are satiating and it is difficult to over-consume them. They are extremely low in fat, high in fiber, and help to reduce the risk of heart disease, cancer, adult onset diabetes, and other illnesses. Most of these foods are high in fiber, which binds with cholesterol in the intestines. The fiber and cholesterol are excreted out of the body together without giving the cholesterol the chance to be absorbed into the bloodstream.

Grains include barley, oatmeal, whole wheat, bran, rye, wild rice, kasha, farina, cous-cous, cream of wheat, bulgur, triticale, amaranth, quinoa, millet, buckwheat, and whole grain cornmeal.

Legumes are also a good source of protein. They include lentils, beans (kidney, pinto, lima, black, navy, mung, white, fava, butter), and peas (green, chick, blackeye, split).

Vegetables include tubers (yam, sweet potato, potato), cruciferous family (cauliflower, broccoli, turnip, collard, brussels sprout, kohlrabi, kale), roots (carrot, radish), leaves (spinach, lettuce, watercress), and gourds (squash, pumpkin). The only vegetable that has a significant amount of oil is the olive. Most vegetables have plenty of flavonoids, carotenoids, and other substances that act as antioxidants, improve immunity, and reduce the risk for cancer.

Starches are healthy to eat, but contain less fiber than vegetables, grains, and legumes. Examples include spaghetti, macaroni, noodles, and other types of pasta.

Fruits are composed of simple and complex carbohydrates. They also contain many carotenoids and flavonoids. Add water to juice to dilute the high concentration of sugar. Consume dried fruits in small portions since they are also high in sugar. The only fruits containing fat are coconuts (saturated) and avocados (similar to olives, the oil is monounsaturated).

Water, diluted fruit juices, vegetable juices, and herbal teas are healthy beverage options. Green tea is recommended since it contains the natural flavonoid antioxidants catechin and epicatechin.

Eat in moderation

Soy beans are the main ingredient in *tofu* (bean curd). Although high in fat (surprisingly, 30-50% of the calories in tofu are fat), tofu contains substances called *genistein* and *daidzein* that may block cancer formation.

Seafood, especially cold-water fish, are fine choices. They contain the long-chain polyunsaturated fatty acids *Omega-3s*. Known as *eicosapentanoic acid* (EPA) and *docosahexanoic acid* (DHA), these fatty acids make the blood's platelets less likely to stick together. This reduces the risk of a coronary artery blockage and heart attack. Good sources of omega-3s are salmon, halibut, tuna, trout, and mackerel. Eat fish at least once a week. If you don't like fish, take fish oil capsules containing EPA and DHA.

Dairy products are okay if eaten in moderation. Preferable to whole milk and cheese are lowfat and fat free milk, cheese, and yogurt.

Chicken and turkey contain large amounts of fat in the skin. Broiling and baking are better means of preparation than frying.

Egg yolks are high in cholesterol. Egg whites consist mostly of protein.

Oils, such as flax, hemp, soybean, safflower, and sunflower, are good sources of essential fatty acids. If you have a low intake of oils, take an additional teaspoon to tablespoon per day. Use unrefined oils, keep them refrigerated, and avoid exposing them to light, air, or high-temperature cooking.

Nuts, except chestnuts, are high in fat.

Sweets and sweeteners such as honey, syrup (maple, corn), molasses, jams, jellies, and sugar are not harmful if eaten in small quantities.

Discouraged (don't be mad at me if these are your favorites)
If your diet is usually healthy, you needn't worry about the occasional consumption (in small portions) of the following foods:

Fats and fried foods such as lard, shortening, butter, margarine, mayonnaise, french fries, potato chips, cream soups, and refined oils (especially hydrogenated). For salad dressing, try fat free or lowfat alternatives. Fat substitutes such as *Simplesse*, maltodextrin, polydextrose, and *Oatrim* appear to be safe.

Meats including sausage, luncheon meat, veal, pork, bacon, liver, hot-dogs, ham, lamb, veal, and organ meats. Lean beef in small portions is okay. *Fowl* to avoid include duck and goose.

Desserts such as pie, cake, cookie, eclair, donut, custard, etc.

Soft drinks, which are high in sugar and caffeine and have no nutritional value. The phosphoric acid may predispose some individuals to dental caries. Furthermore, they are substitutes for healthy drinks.

Physical activity (pressing buttons on your remote control doesn't count)
Even with the perfect diet, full energy and vigor will not be enjoyed if we lead sedentary lives. The benefits of physical activity cannot be overstated. Toned muscles make routine movement, from typing to climbing stairs, effortless. Muscles were meant to be used and kept active. Humans have a natural, inherent need *to move!*

Physical activity adds a few months to a few years to lifespan. According to *Center for Disease Control* statistics, physically active individuals are less likely than their inactive counterparts to develop heart disease, high blood pressure, non-insulin dependent diabetes, osteoporosis, breast cancer, colon cancer, and mental health problems. Choose one or more activities that you enjoy such as running, walking, bicycling, swimming, aerobics, weight-training, yoga, softball, basketball, and martial arts.

Light activities such as walking or gardening twenty minutes a day, a few days a week, are enough to maintain health and longevity. Competing in marathons and *sweating to exhaustion* are not necessary. In fact, over-exercising releases an excess of adrenaline and cortisol into the bloodstream, depressing various components of the immune system. Olympians and other highly trained athletes report an increased frequency of colds after intense training and competition. Because over-exercising is likely to be an oxidative stress on cells, leading to free radical formation, athletes may benefit from taking extra vitamins, especially the antioxidants. Furthermore, excessive caloric consumption places a burden on the cells detoxifying the byproducts of metabolism, resulting in even more free radicals.

Just like other activities, exercise can be performed with tension or enjoyed in a relaxed manner. While playing tennis we can play calmly, enjoy the experience and not worry about winning or losing… or we can tense up and throw fits *a la McEnroe*. The release of adrenaline in the bloodstream speeds heart rate. There is no need to release additional adrenaline from self-induced stress.

Stretch a few minutes before and after exercising. The best kind of stretch is a 'static' stretch. Gradually increase the stretch without straining the muscles by holding the position for ten to twenty seconds. It's best not to start any type of exercise at full speed. Allow time for warm up. After the activity, cool down in order to release the accumulated lactic acid and ketones that cause cramps.

If you experience severe or persistent muscle pain, spasm, or swelling after a workout, your body is telling you to take a break and rest. Neglecting this warning can result in muscle, ligament, and tendon damage, requiring weeks or months for recovery.

If you've been sedentary your entire life avoid the impulse to enthusiastically shovel your neighbors' driveways after a heavy snow fall. The risk for heart attack increases when an out of shape individual attempts a sudden exertion.

Within four to eight months of stopping exercise, a person's fitness level returns to the equivalent of never having been on an exercise program. The following are some overall benefits of physical activity:

•   Better psychological outlook: mood-raising endorphins are stimulated, mental functioning and memory improve, stress and anxiety are reduced, premenstrual depression and anxiety are alleviated.

- The delta (deep) phase of sleep lengthens. To improve sleep, walk or work-out a half-hour in the evening, but not too close to bedtime.

- Agoraphobia (fear of open spaces) and claustrophobia (fear of closed spaces) symptoms are lessened.

- Body image and self-esteem are enhanced. Exercise makes us more comfortable with our bodies and sexuality.

- Body weight is reduced since more calories are expended than are taken in. Abdomen becomes firmer. Thyroid metabolism is enhanced resulting in better weight control.

- Heart muscle grows stronger and pumps a greater volume of blood to the body. Blood pressure decreases. Arteries become elastic and blood capillaries in muscles enlarge.

- Muscle strength, flexibility, and endurance increase. Tendons become more elastic. Bones are less likely to develop osteoporosis.

I was a fourth year medical student completing my surgical rotation at Thomas Jefferson Medical School when a fifty-six year old woman was admitted for hip fracture. She was an author of non-fiction books. While cooking in her kitchen, she slipped on a wet spot and landed on her right hip. Exercise had not been a part of her life. She remarked, "Whenever I get the urge to exercise, I lie down until the thought passes away." Her x-rays revealed that her bones were osteoporotic and brittle. A simple fall to the ground does not cause fractures in strong bones.

A surgeon reunited the fractured hip. The two days following the surgery went well. Unfortunately, on the third day, she became acutely short of breath. She had developed a blood clot in one of the large veins of her right leg. This clot traveled to the lungs and caused a massive pulmonary infarction (the blood supply to a section of her lung was completely cut off). She was placed on a respirator but tragically died a few days later.

Along with her family I grieved her loss. I feel sad whenever a tragedy happens to someone, especially if it could have been easily prevented. It's likely that she would have had much stronger bones, better balance, and a reduced chance of fracture upon falling had she exercised regularly. Exercise and good calcium intake throughout life place a dense reserve of bone in place, buffering bone thinning consequences of osteoporosis.

Our well-being and longevity are influenced by so many factors. Completely neglecting one of these, such as physical activity, can have devastating consequences.

Sleep… the balm that soothes harsh labor's sores

Have you ever awakened from a long, restful sleep and felt completely rejuvenated? The beneficial influence of sleep on health and happiness is often overlooked.

During my internship I learned of the enormous impact of sleep irregularity and deprivation on the body and psyche. For a whole year my medical rotations involved working thirty-four hour shifts every fourth day. This meant I would come in to the hospital at 8 am and work continuously until 6 pm the following day. It was possible to take short naps overnight if there were no emergencies or patient admissions.

After a few months on this routine, I noticed some disturbing changes. I had difficulty concentrating. My ability to learn lessened. My sex drive diminished dramatically. I found myself moody, irritable, and impatient. I felt constantly tired. I started catching colds and sore throats. My relationships and friendships deteriorated. The lack of sleep even took its toll on my empathy for the sick.

One night at 4 am, while napping after a long and arduous day and evening, I was called out of my sleep for a possible admission of a patient to the cardiac unit. The patient had been brought to the emergency room with a massive heart attack and was undergoing cardiopulmonary resuscitation by the emergency room physician. If he survived, he would be taken to the cardiac intensive care unit for observation and I would have to spend an hour or two writing admission orders. As I forced myself awake and put on my white coat, I remember thinking, "Maybe he won't survive and I can go back to sleep." At that point it suddenly hit me. "What am I thinking? I can't believe I placed the importance of my sleep ahead of the life of an individual!" I realized the enormous negative effect– on judgment and empathy, to say the least– of sleep deprivation.

Adequate sleep is vital to learning and memory. Inadequate sleep causes multiple psychological disturbances, interferes with immunity, and decreases lifespan. A consequence of compromised immunity is reduced effectiveness of natural killer cells (the lymphocytes responsible for recognizing and destroying malignant and virus-infected cells). Workers who frequently change their schedules, alternating between day and night shifts, are more likely to succumb to heart attacks, ulcers, infections, and other illnesses. Anyone who has cared for an infant or done shift work truly understands the value of sleep.

The science of sleep

When individuals are isolated in a chamber or cave for a period of weeks without knowledge of time, they tend to go to bed at 24½-hour intervals. In other words, if bedtime the first evening is at midnight, the following night it will be 12:30 am, 1:00 am the following night, and so on. Of course, each person is different. Some individuals have an internal clock of less than twenty-four hours *(larks)* while others may be up to twenty-six or more *(owls)*. A person who is alert in the evenings and has difficulty falling asleep may have a long cycle– and a reflexive urge to flatten the early morning grating, buzzing, alarm clock with a mace. A person who wakes up naturally early in the morning and is sleepy in the evening has a cycle less than twenty-four hours. The blind have cycles similar to people who are isolated in caves or chambers.

The circadian rhythm is controlled by a region in the brain called the *hypothalamus,* specifically the suprachiasmatic nucleus. The hypothalamus communicates with the pineal gland, instructing it to release *melatonin,* the sleep hormone. Beginning in the evening, and continuing through the night, the pineal gland releases melatonin. The peak levels are between 2 and 4 am.

Morning exposure to sunlight resets our biological clock. Photons from sunlight enter through the eyes and stimulate the rods and cones in the retina. This electrical/chemical information is relayed to the hypothalamus and the pineal gland. Morning exposure to sunlight shuts off melatonin release by the pineal.

Exercise has the tendency to shorten the sleep cycle. I'm a night person; my mind is often active past midnight. However, whenever I go on an extended bicycle trip which involves riding all day long, my clock shortens to less than twenty-four hours. I go to bed sooner and wake up bright and early. One possible cause of insomnia in our culture is the physically sedentary yet mentally active lives lead by white collar workers. When bedtime comes the physical body is not exhausted and the mind is still twirling with a whirlwind of thoughts. Contrast this to prior centuries when farmers and laborers were exposed to plenty of light and heavy exertion while working in the field from dawn till dusk. It's likely they slept deeply.

Helpful hints on improving sleep
Go to bed only when you are sleepy. Use your bed only to have sex or sleep. Minimize eating, drinking, and watching television in bed.

Unless a bedroom is completely soundproof there are a variety of noises which disturb a deep sleep. These noises may include a dog barking; a roommate snoring; street noises such as cars, motorcycles, trucks, and police sirens; a slammed door; the hum of the refrigerator, heater or air conditioner; or a plane flying overhead. These noises may not necessarily awaken you, but could shift a profound, restful sleep to one that is shallow and fragmented without your conscious realization. This is likely to interfere with daytime energy and concentration. Invest in soundproof windows or cover them with heavy drapes. Use ear plugs to muffle these noises. I use them every night, and sleep so profoundly!

Consider wearing eye shades while sleeping if light enters your bedroom in the morning. We have the tendency to awaken at dawn when sunlight slips through the shades. After this interruption sleep may not be as restful. Once you are out of bed, expose yourself to a few minutes of sunlight to reset the biological clock. Try to wake up at the same time each morning in order for your body to acquire a consistent sleep rhythm.

Unless you are depended upon for emergencies, turn off your phone at night and turn it back on in the morning. It's a shame waking up in the middle of the night or early morning because of a wrong phone call.

Taking long naps, especially after 4 pm, could make you less sleepy at bedtime.

When body temperature is raised in late afternoon or early evening, it will fall at bedtime, facilitating sleep. A brisk walk, aerobic exercise, or hot bath will serve this purpose. Exercise within two or three hours before bedtime may make you more alert, interfering with slumber.

Caffeine (sodas, chocolate, coffee, certain teas) is best avoided after dinner. Caffeine stimulates the alertness center in the brain. Consumption of alcohol in the evening may help one fall asleep, but the sleep is often fragmented and light. Alcohol suppresses the *delta phase,* physiologically the deepest stage of sleep, as well as REM, the dream state.

Drinking large amounts of fluids in the evening may prompt a middle of the night visit to the bathroom. Eating a late night snack promotes sleep, especially if it is a carbohydrate meal (such as pasta). The carbohydrate stimulates insulin release which promotes the entry of blood *tryptophan* (an amino acid) into the brain. Tryptophan is converted into serotonin, then melatonin, inducing a calm sleep. In order to stay alert during the day, breakfast and lunch should be started with protein.

Strenuous mental activity should stop at least an hour before sleep. Switch the mind to reading or watching a comedy film or TV show. Do chores around the house, take a shower, floss and brush your teeth.

If you occasionally have difficulty sleeping, try a natural sleep aid. *Melatonin* pills are available in health food stores. This is the same melatonin secreted by our pineal gland. Improved sleep occurs when taking a pill an hour or so before bed. A dose of 0.5 mg to 6 mg is effective. As we age, less melatonin is secreted at night. Seniors may benefit most from supplements. Melatonin enhances the immune system and is a powerful antioxidant. It may protect against cancer and age-related loss of neurons. In one study laboratory mice lived twenty percent longer when given melatonin starting in middle age. Most users report vivid dreams. For more details on the fascinating aspects of this supplement please see *Melatonin: Nature's Sleeping Pill.*

Once in bed take all cares and worries off your mind. Lying on your back, shake and loosen a leg and foot. Take a few slow, deep breaths by expanding your belly. Proceed to shake and loosen the other leg and foot and then return to your abdomen for a few more relaxed breaths. Proceed with this relaxation to your arms, shoulders, and neck. Now relax your facial muscles, especially those around the eyes and mouth. Remember to return to slow, abdominal breathing after relaxing each muscle group. Before you know it you'll be drifting into your *adventure-filled* unconscious.

But what if Sleep chuckles and rejects your premature attempt at pillow peace?

When turbulent thoughts
as unwelcome guests
deny still night's
tranquil rest
and restless body bare
acquaints mattress's
every square
perhaps it's best
to play solitaire
or read Moliere
why not a measure
of Debussy's La Mer?

Returning to bed
cares and worries shed
breathe deep the air
eyelids weighty with lead
twiddle your toes
breathe out the air
twiddle your nose
dream of tides and sand
and off you goes
to la la land.

Dreams

An average adult dreams at least once every ninety minutes (five to six times during the night). The duration of these dreams increases over the course of the night, from about five to ten minutes at the end of the first ninety minute sleep cycle to about forty-five minutes at the end of the last. On average, people recall dreams one out of every two nights.

Dreams reflect our desires, grandiose ideas, sexual orientation, fears, and emotional states. Fear of an upcoming exam may be expressed in a dream where you may find it impossible to write on the test sheet; there is no ink in the pen or your hand is paralyzed. If you have been reprimanded for being late to work you may dream of being stuck in a traffic jam with exits blocked. A person uncomfortable with his or her body may dream running through a street without clothes. A budding actor may dream of starring in a successful film.

Many researchers think that dreams serve the purpose of dealing with issues we have not dealt with properly during our waking hours. Recurrent dreams allow us to confront and solve problems that we have been avoiding. If the intensity of the suppressed emotion is strong enough the dream will be intense enough to wake us. By remembering the dream our unconscious mind is signaling us to focus on this issue and resolve it. Dreams also incorporate sensations experienced during the night. If the bedroom temperature becomes very warm, we may dream of a sauna or a hot tropical day. Some noises are also incorporated into a dream. Do all dreams have meaning? Are some dreams due to a random firing of neurons? We're not fully sure.

Dreams will be unpleasant if we harbor anger, grudges, envy, or other negative emotions. By fulfilling the many essentials in this book our dreams will be more agreeable. Dreams are intimately intertwined with psychological health.

Stress

Stress has definite harmful biological effects, whether *physical* (intense athletic competition, illness) or *psychological* (relationship difficulties, financial problems). Our immune system responds quickly to our thoughts and emotions. There are receptors on the surface of white blood cells to which hormones and neurotransmitters can attach. When under stress, substances released by the brain attach to the cells of the immune system and disturb its proper functioning. Positive thoughts and emotions are believed to enhance the immune system. The immune system can in turn send substances back to the brain altering the release of neurotransmitters, thus influencing mood. This is one aspect of the brain-body connection discussed in the appendix.

Luckily we can do something about stress. Much of it is self-induced or self-aggravated. While stuck in traffic we may boil with frustration or turn on the radio and sing along with the songs. Most of our stress is not necessarily due to external circumstances. Rather it is due to our underdeveloped coping skills.

In the 1960s researchers Holmes and Rahe published a list of major life stresses. The top twelve, from the most stressful to the least stressful, were death of a spouse, divorce, marital separation, jail term, death of a close family member, personal injury or illness, marriage, getting fired from a job, marital reconciliation, retirement, change in health of a family member, and pregnancy. However, recent evidence indicates that in the long run, daily hassles and frustrations cause more physical and mental harm than infrequent major life stresses.

How we handle stress— our personality and coping style— is more important than the nature of the stress. One spouse may find divorce a relief while the other is devastated. A downturn of the stock market may be shrugged off by one investor while causing a coronary in another. How do you react to unpleasant circumstances? Are you upset by every little thing throughout the day that doesn't go according to your plans, or do you calmly adapt to unplanned situations?

Consequences of stress include:

1. *Immune system malfunction making us more susceptible to colds, various infections, and recurrent herpes attacks.* The following is one example of how stress leads to infections. The lining of our mucous membranes (mouth, throat, lung, intestines) is occupied by various germs.

They are prevented from entering our bodies partly by immune globulins coating our mucous membranes. Mental stress induces the pituitary gland to release ACTH which goes into the bloodstream, travels to the adrenal gland, and prompts it to release cortisol. The release of cortisol inhibits the function of immune globulins. This makes it easier for bacteria or viruses to enter our bodies and cause infections.

2. *Increased risk of heart disease, high blood pressure, and stroke.* Platelets clot faster. This leads to atherosclerosis, blood clots, and heart attacks.

3. *Backaches, neckaches, chronic fatigue syndrome, muscle tension, along with various gastrointestinal symptoms such as belching, irritable bowel syndrome, belly aches, and stomach ulcers.*

4. *Increased likelihood of depression, anxiety, panic attacks, arguments, and relationship difficulties.* Decreased sex drive and enjoyment of life are common consequences of prolonged stress. Even pain in sexual organs has been reported.

5. *Have you ever had difficulty learning while going through a tension filled period in your life?* Stress hormones, such as cortisol, cause dendrites– the branches of neurons that receive signals from adjacent neurons– to shrink in the hippocampus, a brain region involved in learning and memory. Too much stress can even kill neurons.

6. *Stress has even been linked to an increased incidence of cancer.* In some studies individuals had a higher incidence of breast cancer if unable to externalize their emotions and obtain appropriate help and counseling. Bottling up emotions damages the immune system.

The first step in dealing with stress is to identify its source. Next, take specific action to relieve or eliminate it. Take a moment, now or later, and list any stresses in your current life in a private journal. Beside it write how you plan to deal with them.

There are times when life is cruel and our load is so heavy that we just want to sit and cry. That's perfectly okay. Crying helps to wash away toxic chemicals and hormones built up during stress, improving mood. It's healthy to cry once in a while.

There are many ways to relieve stress: vacations, playing with pets, improving sleep and physical health, finding satisfying work, establishing financial security, and participating in meditation and yoga. Let's not underestimate the benefits of positive mental attitude– it's not what happens to us, it's what we make of it.

Relaxation, meditation, and yoga

Many of us lead rushed lives. The annoying blare of the alarm clock rouses us from a mid-REM dream as we rush to the bathroom to shower and make our faces presentable. We don clothes that could have used a few more passes with the iron, gulp down breakfast, and stuff our throats with half-chewed cereal. Already a few minutes late, we rush to the car, race to the office to juggle phone calls, meetings, and conversations. Our breathing is shallow, irregular. We are holding our breath.

Why rush? Everything we do throughout the day can be accomplished just as well in a relaxed manner. Rushing only shaves a few seconds from each activity while preventing us from enjoying them. By relaxing, we can enjoy routine activities such as dressing, dialing the phone, tying shoe laces, and heating water for tea. The unhurried Japanese tea ceremony indicates that a simple activity such as sipping tea can be developed into an art form.

Taking a few minutes from our hectic schedules to relax and clear our thoughts is difficult. Something is usually churning in our heads. We have telephone calls to return, appointments to keep, uncompleted projects, a recent interaction to ruminate on. Relaxation and meditation techniques can teach us to become conscious of our body rhythms, especially our breath. They can help us find an oasis of peace within ourselves. It is always there; we just need to connect with it.

Throughout the day if you notice yourself tense or irritable, take a moment to unwind with a deep breath followed by a slow exhalation. Continue being aware of the air slowly expanding your abdomen. You may find breathing through your abdomen more relaxing than expanding your chest. As you repeat this process, you will become calmer. Imagine a balmy breeze soothing your refreshed soul while you unwind under the cool palm tree shade of a tropical isle.

The following are simple steps to serenity: find a quiet place at home or in the office; use ear plugs if needed. Sit comfortably in a chair or on the floor. (Some prefer lying down, but it may lead to napping.) Close your eyes. Tighten and relax each muscle from crown to sole. Concentrate on your breath, remembering to breathe slowly and deeply, expanding the belly. Breathe through your nose. As you breathe out, say the word 'one' silently to yourself. For the next ten to thirty minutes continue concentrating on your breathing. Acknowledge any thoughts that come to your mind, and let them travel on.

Yoga, a system of poses that promotes awareness of mind and body, began as a Hindu discipline to train consciousness for spiritual insight and tranquillity. In our culture it is practiced mostly for its physical benefits. If you have never tried yoga, I highly recommend taking a course or attending a few sessions. Take at least two or three different classes since each instructor will have a different style– you may find a significant difference in how you feel from each style, and each class.

If done properly yoga is one of the most simultaneously relaxing and invigorating activities one can do. Yoga teaches flexibility and balance. Using the entire body and mind, yoga creates a profound sense of well-being and tranquillity. Reduced stress and enhanced self-awareness are benefits that carry over into other life pursuits. It's difficult to describe with words how good a few classes of yoga can make one feel.

My experience with yoga started with a four day course between the Christmas and New Year holiday at the *Kripalu Center for Yoga and Health* in Lenox, Massachusetts. As part of the program, we were not allowed to speak the first three days. There were three yoga classes interspersed throughout the day, the first one starting at 5 am. The meals consisted of delicious vegetarian dishes of grains and cereals garnished with a variety of vegetables and condiments. We all ate in a large dining room, but no one spoke. It was so strange. I had never eaten with a group of people in complete silence. Even stranger was the fact that I was beginning to enjoy this quiet. Instead of being involved in a conversation and constantly thinking, listening and replying, I realized how relaxing it was to just focus on nothing but the taste of food. I began to be aware of my arm movement as the fork shuttled the rice from the plate to my mouth. I then noticed the chewing process, something automatic I had never contemplated before. There is so much more to eating that we normally overlook.

In my free time, between eating and the classes, I cross-country skied in the nearby snowy woods, continuing the flow of silence. Each yoga class would relax, limber, and stretch me beyond that which I had experienced before. I felt as rejuvenated and energetic as a child who has not yet learned the word 'fatigue.' I glided on my skis as if the Newtonian laws of friction had been suspended from our planet's surface.

The expected outcome of this four-day yoga course was a total body/mind relaxation. And so it was! What was unexpected began the last day of the course. An overwhelming feeling of well-being and caring began as if the floodgates of universal love had blasted open. I felt peace and love for everything and everyone.

Feeding the brain– be kind to your mind
Everything discussed in this book deals with improving physical and mental health. In this section I wish to explain how we can make our minds even healthier by replacing negative input with positive input.

In recent years we have become aware of the relationship between diet and physical health. Whatever enters our stomach affects our body. We need to be as careful about what enters our mind. Two common sources of negative input that people are exposed to include:

1. *Unhealthy relationships with parents, spouse, lover, relatives, employer, or roommates.* The ego takes a regular beating. Frequent arguments perpetuate disharmony. The constant exposure to this emotional insult inevitably has a detrimental influence on our psyche and consequently affect physical health and happiness. If improving the lines of communication and restoring healthy interactions are not possible it may be appropriate to withdraw temporarily from unhealthy relationships until everyone comes to their senses.

2. *Movies, books, and television programs that portray violence and horror.* It has become quite clear that viewing violence makes children

and teenagers more aggressive. Their dreams are also affected. Radio talk shows that continually criticize and disparage individuals or groups due to ethnic, racial, and sexual orientation are an additional source of negativity.

Let's be conscious of what we feed our minds. Watching excessively violent movies, or reading similar books, is for the mind what consuming junk food is to the body. I had an appalling dream one night. I awoke with a pounding heart and profuse sweating. The dream consisted of two knights in a forest involved in a duel. The knight dressed in white swung an enormous sword slicing off the left arm of the black night. Blood hemorrhaged from the left shoulder. The white knight proceeded to sever the right arm and then the lower extremities... I sat on the edge of my mattress. This was unusual for me; I rarely, if ever, have nightmares. I tried to think of the origin of these images. Two days later, it dawned on me. *Monty Python and the Holy Grail* (released in 1974) was the source. It was a comedy and a hilarious film. I really enjoyed watching the film at the time, but I do remember being repulsed by that scene. The images of the duel, ingrained in my subconscious, returned in a nightmare years after I had seen the movie. If this type of violent but comedic scene was ingrained in my subconscious, one can imagine how much of an impact a true horror film can have, especially on impressionable children.

If you enjoy horror entertainment, I recommend you expose yourself less frequently. Realize that whatever enters your mind will affect your unconscious. Of course each person is different and there may be individuals who are affected very little. They may even have an attitude of acceptance for violence and horror and not be disturbed by it. At night our dreams symbolically replay some of the images exposed in our waking hours. Horror scenes are bound to come up in dreams whether or not we consciously realize it. We know for certain that horror movies cause nightmares in children. Their effect on adults has not been studied as well.

I do not advocate shying away from observing realistic violence. We live in a harsh and sometimes cruel world. We have to adapt to unpleasant reality. If we come across an accident, a murder, or other dreadful setting, we should not turn around and run away. Let's look at it, accept the reality, feel empathy for the victim, help any way we can and embrace our fear, loathing, or repulsion.

Humans have the remarkable capacity to adapt to repugnant events and circumstances. My first semester at medical school involved anatomy lab with dissection of formaldehyde soaked cadavers. The first time I entered the lab I felt nausea creeping up my abdomen. Forty shriveled, ghastly bodies were supine on cold, stark metal tables. The anatomy professor happened to be a spirited and understanding man adept at putting students at ease. After a few days of anatomy lab, dissection became routine and no longer upset me.

I have recounted this anecdote to stress the point that realistic unpleasant events have to be faced and adapted to. Television and newspapers inundate us daily with crime, famines, or civil war conflicts. The proper course of dealing with these images is to observe them, absorb them, and think about them rationally and calmly until they have become familiar. In the end, familiarity blunts their terror. We need to remind ourselves to make a conscious effort not to let familiarity blunt our empathy for victims. However, there is no reason to go out of our way and repeatedly expose ourselves to terrible images once we feel we can calmly deal with them. It is quite possible that in our own lifetime we may personally encounter a fearful event. If we have adapted well, we will manage the impact more calmly. If you are going through a difficult period in your life and already have more problems that you can handle, it may be appropriate to block out all difficult-to-deal-with images until the time stability rules.

As we gain more experience and learn that disagreeable realism will not overwhelm us if we have to face it, there is little reason to keep exposing ourselves to unpleasantness. Concentrate your attention towards permeating your thoughts and senses with cheerfulness and love. Place positive thoughts in your mind. Listen to motivational tapes. Read other self-help books. Watch inspirational films. Watch comedy films and laugh heartily. Collect cartoons and jokes from books and magazines and share them with friends and relatives. Be around positive people who are a good influence on you. Reduce or eliminate complaints and criticisms. By complaining we magnify our discontent. Instead, look at the bright side of things and the positive aspects of people in your daily life.

Visualize yourself as successful in the goals you have set. Repeatedly practice in your mind goals or activities you want to accomplish. Spend time alone in quiet contemplation and come up with new insights. Repeat to yourself the following affirmations: "I love myself." "I am a good person who is constantly getting better." "I deserve to be happy." "My own happiness will improve other peoples' lives."

Why do some people expose themselves to negativity?

People often seek out movies with tragic endings, read books that are depressing, and do other things that seem to contradict a hedonistic motivation. Why? Let's look at some reasons:

1. *To feel 'alive.'* If there aren't exciting events going on in our lives, watching violent or horror films will cause significant arousal. Some people feel better being negatively alive than not alive at all.

2. *To feel better by comparing our lot to those who are worse off or suffering.* We realize our own life isn't that bad.

3. *As a form of catharsis.* When we see others who are going through similar difficult times, we identify with them, and realize we are not alone in suffering. As we empathize with them and cry, we feel better.

4. *To become familiar with tragedy and not let it upset us if we come to experience it ourselves.*

There are more reasons. I just want to point out that when something initially appears to be against our innate human motivation to be as happy as possible, in the end it does serve the purpose of enhancing well-being. It's possible that altruism follows similar logic. By helping others or giving of ourselves we ultimately feel better; some consider this giving an investment leading to future rewards.

Common sense guidelines to long-term health and happiness
Premature illness and death are incompatible with happiness. In 1990 approximately 2,148,000 people in the US died. Half of these deaths were determined to be premature, that is, they could have been postponed. Let's look at some of the causes for premature death in the year 1990 (as reported in the November 10, 1993, *Journal of the American Medical Association):*

tobacco 400,000
poor diet/lack of exercise 300,000
alcohol 100,000
infections 90,000
toxic agents 60,000
firearms 36,000
risky sexual behavior 30,000
auto accidents 25,000
improper use of drugs 20,000.

We'll discuss each of these causes of premature illness and death. (Diet and physical activity were discussed earlier.) These factors may act independently of each other, the risks being simply additive, or they may act synergistically, the interaction of factors presenting a greater total risk than the sum of their individual effects. Each of us can do a great deal to influence our health destiny.

Tobacco– Heart disease and cancer are the nation's leading killers. The biggest underlying cause for these two major illnesses is excessive exposure to cigarette smoke. If you decide now to stop smoking cold turkey, withdrawal symptoms will dissipate in one week. The majority of people who quit do so without external help or devices. If you really want to quit, you can. Nicotine patches or gum can help. Biofeedback also works. As with losing weight, quitting smoking is easier when other sources of pleasures or diversion are found. Boredom, a low mood, being around smokers, can all spark the urge to light up.

In addition to lung cancer, additional harm caused by cigarettes include cancer of esophagus, oral cavity, pancreas, kidney, bladder, cervix, colon, leukemia, and perhaps other sites; emphysema (destruction of lung tissue); frequent colds and bronchitis (the smoke damages the lining of the throat and respiratory system making it more likely for bacteria and viruses to get a foothold); increased risk of cardiovascular disease (coronary artery disease, stroke, high blood pressure); impotence; and skin wrinkling. Smoking is known to cause long-term, but reversible, loss to the sense of smell. Individuals who smoke throughout their lives will, on average, die five to fifteen years earlier than those who never smoke. A *two pack a day* smoker will spend more than 60,000 dollars on cigarettes in a lifetime. Waiters and waitresses have twice the risk of lung cancer as the general population because of their exposure to patrons' smoke. Dogs are twice as likely to get lung cancer when their owners are smokers.

Even though nicotine is addictive, there are smokers– cigarette or pipe– who have the self-guidance to do so infrequently. They enjoy an occasional puff or two at social gatherings or after a meal. An infrequent smoke is unlikely to be harmful.

Alcohol– Small amounts of alcohol are not harmful (and may even be beneficial), but frequent and large consumption lead to liver damage, colon cancer, weakness of the heart muscle, and diminished immune response. Alcohol is also responsible for half of all motor vehicle fatalities. Frequent and regular use interferes with memory and learning. Alcohol suppresses the body's ability to dispose of fat, resulting in the so-called 'beer belly.' Alcoholism, a retreat into analgesic haven, is a slow form of suicide. "'Tis not the drinking to be blamed, but the excess," hiccupped John Selden (1584-1654), the English author, while tavern-hopping.

Microbial Agents– The major contributors to death from infectious agents are pneumococcal pneumonia, legionellosis, staphylococcus, hepatitis, and group A streptococcus. If we follow a healthy lifestyle and get proper immunizations our primed immune system will launch more effective artillery and missiles against any germs that insist on invading our bodies, setting up camp, and annoying our white blood cells.

Toxic agents are the synthetic chemicals and environmental pollutants that we are exposed to through occupational hazards. Additional exposure occurs through contaminants in food and water. Avoid processed foods loaded with chemicals. Wash off pesticides from vegetables and fruits. Air pollution (carbon monoxide, sulfur dioxide, lead, particulate matter) and geophysical factors (background ionizing radiation and ultraviolet light) are also factors in cancer causation.

Excessive sun exposure, especially between the hours of 10 am and 3 pm, causes skin damage, wrinkling, suppression of immune function, herpes outbreak (cold sore), and skin cancer. Prolonged sun exposure also accelerates the process of cataract (dark areas in the lens causing blindness) formation in the eye. Use sunglasses and shields. Tanning salons use UV-A light that can cause skin damage. Sunscreens do not offer complete protection from skin cancer.

If you're over thirty, apply Retin-A 0.05% cream to your face two or three times a week to slow the process of wrinkling or sun damage (consult your physician). A diet high in carotenes, flavonoids, and other antioxidants can partially negate the detrimental effects of sun exposure.

Firearms– We have a frightening crime rate in our country. Yearly, firearms cause 16,000 murders, 19,000 suicides, and 1,400 accidental killings. Compare these numbers to the rare occurrence of firearm deaths in many European countries. England usually has less than a dozen a year. The risk of suicide among adolescents is three times greater in homes where a gun is kept. Guns kept in homes as protection are three times more likely to kill a family member than an intruder.

We can reduce the chance of accidents or being a victim of a crime by staying vigilant and aware of our surroundings. The highest risk for being assaulted is between midnight and 6 am. Alcohol ingestion dramatically increases this risk. We don't live in a perfect world; we may fall prey to unscrupulous or criminally-minded individuals if we are not careful. Feeling universal love for humankind does not grant us immunity from this. "Yield not thy neck to fortune's yoke," cautioned Shakespeare, "but let thy dauntless mind still ride in triumph over all mischance."

Risky sexual behavior– In 1990, 4,000 women died of cervical cancer (promiscuity without using a condom or cervical cap increases the risk of cervical cancer due to the papilloma virus). Sexually acquired hepatitis B killed 1,600; 21,000 died of HIV. The number of AIDS deaths is likely to increase in the 1990's. Wear a condom.

Motor Vehicles– If you live in a snowy or rainy climate, purchase a car with an airbag and anti-lock braking system (ABS). Wearing a lap and shoulder belt doubles one's chance of survival.

Relax while driving. Leave for your destination early so as not to be in a rush. Put lots of space between you and the car in front of you. Most accidents are preventable and occur in predictable patterns. The following are the most common cause of accidents: running a red light or stop sign, not yielding, improper passing, driving under the influence of drugs or alcohol, tailgating, speeding, and sleepiness.

Improper use of drugs contributes to deaths for such causes as overdose, suicide, homicide, car fatalities (driving under the influence), and pneumonia. Heroin overuse can cause seizures. Cocaine overuse can lead to cardiac arrhythmia and sudden death. Sharing contaminated needles leads to HIV infection, hepatitis, and endocarditis (infection of a heart valve by bacteria introduced through needles used for injecting the drug into the blood stream).

More common sense guidelines

Noise pollution significantly influences health and mood. Sounds of traffic, road construction, and airplanes affect our overall well-being. In addition to hearing damage, exposure to noxious noise causes aggravation and irritability. People who live near freeways or airports may find themselves miserable. Repeated attendance to rock concerts (with decibel levels up to 110) may permanently damage hearing. Reduce the decibel level of your home stereo, car radio, and headphones. Through the day, use ear plugs to block out any loud or annoying noises. One in ten Americans is a victim of noise pollution on a regular basis. Culprits that contribute to hearing loss include chain saws, household appliances, woodworking tools, lawn care equipment, airplanes, recreational vehicles, and high-volume music sounds measuring above eighty-five decibels. Normal conversation is between sixty-five and seventy decibels.

Michael P. got a cochlear implant after being deaf for 15 years. When interviewed on NBC news he said, "I had forgotten what a noisy world it was. How much there is all around you."

Dental care– Good oral health influences well-being. Brush your teeth and floss at least once a day, especially after dinner or before going to bed. Rinse your mouth with water after meals to dislodge food particles. Gargle with a fluoride mouthwash before going to bed. Visit a dentist twice a year for a checkup and thorough tooth cleaning. If you have a good set of teeth to start with there is no reason not to keep them the rest of our life. With proper care and regular dental visits, the need for fillings, crowns, and root canals, costing thousands of dollars, can be dramatically reduced.

Preventive medicine– Potential diseases can be caught at an early stage and treated appropriately by taking advantage of preventive medicine. Regular exams and some tests are especially appropriate for those who have a family history of heart disease, high blood pressure, cancer, or hereditary conditions. Consult your physician.

Almost everything discussed in this book involves the acquiring of knowledge and its implementation. The following chapter discusses how we can learn *how to learn*, expand our brain capacity, and reap the far-reaching benefits of mind expansion.

BE HAPPIER STARTING NOW

NINE

Learning and Creating

It is not enough to have a good mind.
The main thing is to use it well.
Rene Descartes (1596-1650)
French philosopher and mathematician

Continually expanding our minds through learning and creativity is crucial to successful adaptation to this ever-changing informational society. Knowledge helps us advance in our career, leading to higher income, greater travel and leisure opportunities, less stress, more autonomy... and more *happiness*. Being relaxed and happy is a prerequisite for love to grow.

A large fund of knowledge gives us an increased sense of self-confidence. As our topics of interest and discussion increase, the number and variety of friends increase proportionally. Knowledge also improves our ability to foresee future political, economic, and historical trends. Improved understanding of history and cultures wipes clean the dusty lenses of prejudice.

The more we learn, the more we wish to continue learning. Understanding the world is like a jigsaw puzzle. The more pieces fitted in, the clearer the image, and the greater the urge to learn and fill in even more pieces. Increasing knowledge can be compared to an avalanche. Once the process starts, it gathers momentum of its own. Perseverance and some initial prompting are required, but the rewards soon pay off. Minds are kept young by continual use. Mentally active people live longer. *Learning is as important to our brain as exercise is to our body.* It is true that we use only a fraction of our brain's capacity. "Do you realize that most people use two percent of their mind's potential?" asked Crystal on the TV show *Roseanne*. "That much, huh?" was the reply. I consider learning to be a lifelong process. The march of intellect need not halt soon after framing the high school or college sheepskin.

The human brain is infinitely more complex than a computer. The brain is made of living tissue that has the ability to restructure itself. You can improve your brain's memory, creativity, and intelligence by your own conscious effort and freewill. Even though our brain is made of nerve tissue, it can be compared to muscle. The brain has the ability to develop and improve the more it's used. Researchers at the University of California, Los Angeles, studied the brains of twenty dead people. They examined the dendrites (tree-like communicating arms between neurons) and found that the length of dendrites increased proportionally to a person's education and lifestyle. Those with a college education and a mentally active life had longer dendrites than those with less education and an intellectually sedentary lifestyle. Animal studies also seem to confirm the *use it or lose it* theory. Rats placed in an enriched environment (maze learning) show an increase in dendritic growth and enhanced problem-solving ability. They form new synapses between neurons. This facilitates learning even more. When they were moved to an impoverished environment, dendritic material decreased, and synapses regressed. Neurons can grow and change through the last hours of life.

Physical activity improves mental function. Exercise induces growth of capillaries (tiny blood vessels) in the brain. The aging process leads to a decrease in blood supply to the brain. Exercise throughout life buffers against senescence associated decrease in mental function.

While in medical school, I was presented with an enormous amount of information to learn and memorize. During vacation time, I shied away from reading or learning non-medical topics. I had the mistaken notion that the brain had limited capacity, and believed that anything else that I learned would take away valuable space. I have since discovered otherwise. The brain has virtually unlimited capacity to absorb and retain information, but demands stimulation. A physically inactive person is unable to easily complete a three mile running race. After weeks or months of training, three miles will seem like a warm-up. Likewise, the brain gets into shape the more it is used.

The more we learn, the more aspects of life we can be aware of, appreciate, and enjoy. As an example, I remember spending a day bird-watching in a Malibu, California, nature preserve. With the help of an ornithologist, I learned to identify sandpipers, terns, curlews, pelicans, egrets, and several types of seagull. Each time I walk on a beach, or am amongst nature, I am much more aware of the birds I'm sharing with.

Here are some practical recommendations in accumulating a broad knowledge base. Learning is an art. *Let's learn how to learn.*

Look up unfamiliar words in the dictionary. Jot a reminder by the word to indicate where you encountered it, whether it be a book, a newspaper, or in conversation. As an example, if you came across a new word in *The New York Times,* write NYT by the word in the dictionary. If your professor, Ms. Plotnik, mentioned it, write her name by the word. If you came across it in this book, put a smile, or a heart with a smile, next to it. Next time you look up the same word, the previous annotation will help you form an association and you will remember the word better. There are so many occasions when I look up a word in my dictionary and realize I have noted it before. I make a special effort to remember this word in order to learn it once and for all. The odds are high that I will encounter this word again in the future. I often do. Crossword puzzles are a great way to exercise the mind and learn new words.

Once we start learning new words it is a pleasant surprise when we encounter the same words again. Each new word becomes a personal friend, reinforcing a memory. Consider the dictionary one of your most interesting friends. The more words we learn, the more aware we become of our surroundings. Words enrich our memory. "Words form the thread on which we string our experiences," summarized Aldous Huxley (1894-1963), the British philosopher.

Buy an atlas and study the names of the US states, major countries in the world, and their capitals. Learn the names of large cities, bodies of water, mountains, and deserts. Learning geographical names is not as difficult as it sounds. If you concentrate for an hour or two, you can memorize all the capitals in Europe. When you come across an unfamiliar geographical name, look it up in an atlas. When you meet a person from a foreign country, look for the country on a map and read its history. A brief history of every country can be found in a world almanac or encyclopedia. Next time you see this person, share what you learned. Learning the history and current events of a particular country has increased my empathy for the hardships many individuals experience during their migration to the USA. I have come across many Iranis who escaped from Iran by perilously crossing high mountains into Afghanistan. Each of them has a fascinating story to tell.

"In order to understand the present, you must study the past," advised Polybius (208-126 BCE), the Greek historian. It's true. Read a concise history of Western civilization from Egyptian, Babylonian, Greek, and Roman times through the Middle Ages, Renaissance, Age of Reason, American and French revolutions, First and Second World Wars, and up to the modern epoch. This will enhance your understanding of current world events. Recent events in Yugoslavia are understood more clearly when the history of the region is studied from medieval times to the present. A good understanding of American history and politics is necessary in order to become an informed citizen. In this age of cross-culturalism, a basic knowledge of African, Asian, South and Central American history is helpful. "Our ignorance of history causes us to slander our own times," marked Gustave Flaubert (1821-1880), the French novelist. Before we speak harshly of our own country, political system, and all the other imperfections in society, we need to place them in perspective. Knowledge of history makes us realize how unjust ruling systems have been in the past and how much we have advanced, especially since the American and French revolutions. Our present society is part of an evolutionary process. Hopefully, the trend will continue towards an ever more equitable system.

News has been defined as "the first rough draft of history." Stay informed enough to have a good comprehension of current events. We have to be aware of local, state, national, and international developments. In some cases these events may affect us personally– if not in the present, then possibly somewhere down the line.

Learn the basics of human anatomy and physiology. The elementary medical knowledge you obtain will be useful if you ever require the services of a doctor or hospital. You will be able to better understand your diagnosis. Keeping up with the advances of medical technology and research will also be easier.

Invest in a computer. It will help you organize and store information that is important and interesting to you. Use the word processor to help you write articles, letters, essays, etc. The organization of the paragraphs, sections and chapters in this book was made possible by a computer originally purchased for my medical practice. Two or three months after the purchase, I began to see its usefulness in writing. Word-processing is only the beginning. You can find so many other uses. Instead of buying birthday or holiday cards, use your computer to create your own. People will appreciate your effort in creating something personal.

If you're a college student, take advantage of the opportunity to expand your mind. Take every course seriously even if you can't see its practical use. You never know when the information will be useful. Incorporate this knowledge into your long-term memory. Cramming can be compared to a computer's RAM– soon forgotten when the computer is off or the test is over. If you're not sure what to major in, take a variety of courses and learn each subject well. The more knowledge you accumulate, the clearer will become your eventual goal or niche. Become an expert in a particular field which holds your passion. If you're fortunate, this will also be your source of income.

There is so much to learn! Life is enriched by having a basic understanding of world religions, Greek and Roman mythology, art, music, American, British and world literature, business and economics, psychology, sociology, politics, and the sciences.

A good TV show to watch is *Jeopardy!* The game is a great mental exercise improving memory and recall. One can learn an incredible amount of useful information. I have programmed my VCR to tape each evening's show. Once a week, I sit down to review all the episodes. Each time I come across a word, person, or fact that I don't know, I jot it down and then look it up in a reference book. There have been countless occasions where I've learned something new from the show. Soon thereafter, I have come across it again. During one episode, I learned the name of a French dish, *Coquille St. Jacques* (scallops in a white creamy sauce).

Two days later, this dish was mentioned during the television coverage of the 1992 Winter Olympics in Albertville, France. The television reporter stood knee-deep in snow in front of a charming alpine restaurant when I heard him say, "I've just had a most delicious *Coquille St. Jacques* at this French restaurant..." If I hadn't been familiar with the name of this dish, I would not have understood what he had meant. A few months before this book was published, I was at an ocean-front seafood restaurant at Half Moon Bay, CA, when I came across this dish on the menu. I ordered it and was it delicious!

The key to learning and remembering is organizing the information. Start with a three-ringed notebook. Each page can deal with a different topic such as art, botany, gems, meteorology, music, physics, etc. List the topics in alphabetical order. Each time you encounter a new word, you can write it on the appropriate page and then organize it further on a word processor as the pages get filled. The acquisition of knowledge and understanding has been one of the most rewarding experiences of my life. It has resulted in financial security, satisfying work, improved health, an ability to relate to varied peoples, and the sense of confidence necessary to write this book. The more we know, the more control we have over the course and direction of our lives. Knowledge also makes life more meaningful. According to the Roman playwright Seneca (4 BCE-65 ACE), "A good mind possesses a kingdom."

We can be smarter and more creative than we are now. Learning is a joy. Knowledge is a friend. Francis Bacon (1561-1626), the English philosopher, wrote, "Knowledge is power." We can use the power we acquire through knowledge to improve our lives and that of society. Knowledge leads to progress.

Cultivate your creativity
"The barriers are not erected," wrote Ludwig von Beethoven (1770-1827), the German composer, "which shall say to aspiring talent, 'Thus far and no farther.'"

Creativity, an expression of one's individuality, demands self-discipline, that is, motivation, effort, and perseverance. There is a strong urge in humans to create, construct, or invent. The end product could be a piece of art, a musical score, a poem, a house, an essay, a laboratory project, etc. In addition to the excitement and sense of achievement that creativity brings forth, it is fulfilling to contribute to society. There is ample opportunity for most people to create, at work or at home.

We can find original ways to approach daily problems. An office worker can write a better memo, a secretary can improve the filing system for customer phone numbers, a gardener can model new shapes of bushes, a laboratory worker can find a new solution to a project, a homemaker can find creative ways to shop and balance the family budget, and a musician can create a new melody.

During a creative process, it is best not to compare your work with others. Don't ask, "How can I paint better than Rembrandt?" Don't say, "I can never be as inventive as Edison." Create for yourself– for your own pleasure. Expand and maximize your own potential rather than competing. Your creative possibilities are far more extensive than you recognize. You can create for a specific purpose and goal or for self-gratification. Sometimes we spend too much time watching television (watching the creation of other people) or wasting time at idle activities (due to poor time management). We do not make the necessary effort to produce that which has not existed previously. The concentration involved in a creative process is most fulfilling and meaningful.

You have a great deal of potential if you dedicate yourself. I speak from personal experience. During high school and college, writing and English literature were my least favorite courses. I can't remember ever getting an A or even a B in these classes. In college I was a business major before switching to science and going on to medical school. The extent of my writing for years was medical notes within patient charts. It wasn't until June of 1992 that I began to record some of my thoughts. I never intended to write an entire book. I was only jotting down some of my views to share with friends. My first draft was ten pages. My friend Audrey read it and said, "The ideas are good, why don't you expand on this?" I couldn't think of what more to write, so I put the manuscript aside. I returned to it in November of 1992. A few months later, when I showed her the expanded manuscript of fifty pages, her reaction was, "Boy, you've improved so much. Your initial writing was terrible!" "What?! I thought you said my original draft was good!" I replied, shocked. "I said the ideas were good, I didn't have the guts to tell you the writing was terrible."

Ten pages slowly grew to fifty pages, then became the book you are now holding in your hands. I never thought I had the *ability* to write or create. But with perseverance and effort the writing style refined. I've gone over some sentences dozens of times. I spent between 3000 and 4000 hours on this project, writing, revising, rearranging, thinking, researching, learning how to use a computer, and learning all the details required to self-publish a book. Through persistence, revision, and practice, you can improve your abilities in any field that holds your passion or interest. There are no limits. Creating provides a wonderful, long-lasting feeling. Sprout and cultivate the creative seeds lying dormant in the fallow fields of your imagination. The following are a few suggestions on how to improve creativity.

Have a wide variety of experiences and adventures– fodder to draw from. Improve your attentiveness to daily details. Cultivate a wide range of knowledge in the field you are creating. Spend time alone thinking, reflecting and visualizing. Carry a notepad or tape recorder and jot down or voice any ideas that come to you throughout the day. If an idea or thought is not recorded, there is no guarantee that it will come to your mind again in the future.

Improving self-esteem, letting go of long-time hurts, erasing anger, jealousy, and other negative emotions, will all serve to improve creativity. You will be able to harness the full, undistracted concentration of your brain. Positive feelings such as happiness are more conducive to creativity than sadness. Exercise stimulates certain parts of the creative brain. Good sleep, without question, is essential. Another argument for the importance of a complete approach to happiness.

Whatever you create, there will always be some people who will not appreciate it, and give negative feedback. Take these criticisms as advice. Some of their suggestions may be correct, some not.

Since the first printing of this book I have learned even more about the variety of opinions we humans have. People have so many different perspectives. Here are some comments from readers.

"Your introduction is too scientific. It would be better if you shortened it and made it simpler."

"The introduction was great! You should discuss some of the sections, like the part about brain chemistry, in more detail."

"There's no reason to talk about mood medicines in a book like this."

"The part about Prozac and mood-improving medicines is fascinating. You should discuss them in more detail. This is one of the aspects about this book that makes it so different from the other self-help books written by non-physicians."

One of the hardest decisions for a creator is to know which advice to take and which to ignore.

The best way to begin creating is to start. Yes, start. Begin with anything. Then, over time, you can start revising. Soon you'll be amazed at the progress. Don't underestimate your potential. The brain is an amazing organ.

Now, for a moment, let's go beyond the concept of creativity as something concerning external objects; rather, let's contemplate our whole being, flesh and mind, as a mobile work of art, fluid, malleable, ever-adapting, ever-improving, bathed in inner peace, mirthed in natural harmony, flowing gracefully through time and space, and... as we reach the final chapter, capping our long, fascinating journey into happiness, we'll learn how we can intensify our meaningful purpose in this world. By developing a deeper religious, philosophic, and scientific understanding, we further our appreciation of this wonderful world, this multi-colored mosaic. We begin to connect with the thriving, teeming multitudes of earthlings, each one cherishing an interesting belief, an interesting perspective, a personal truth that we accept and respect, and with whom, as a big family, we share this fantastic, priceless sphere

this emerald splendor
this unique jewel
orbiting the hollow
vastness of the Milky Way.
This green-twirling
azure-robed
sun-glittered globe
we affectionately,
intimately, call
our playground
our garden
our home…
dear Planet Earth.

TEN

Developing a Personal Truth

Say not, "I have found the truth"
but rather, "I have found a truth."
Khalil Gibran

The intent of this chapter is not to shepherd you into any particular belief system, but to present some ideas for you to pursue at your leisure. Even if we are comfortable with our own beliefs, learning about the various religions, philosophies, and scientific viewpoints leads to a deeper understanding and connection with the rest of humankind enabling us to sidestep the 'us *versus* them' mentality. We become wiser when we see the world from multiple perspectives.

We all carry belief systems which attempt to explain the world. They influence our major decisions affecting the course of our lives. We carry a universal or cosmic belief system in order to understand the origin of the universe and the nature of a creator or creative force. This belief is most often influenced by our religious upbringing and our understanding of scientific or philosophic explanations. We also harbor countless little beliefs about details of daily life. Examples include our views on astrology, abortion, social issues, politics, ghosts, miracles, etc. These 'little' beliefs draw an influence from our universal belief system.

A universal belief system is important to develop. It helps to focus our long-term goals giving us a meaning and direction in life. A cause to commit to and dedicate ourselves to is gratifying. We feel a sense of harmony and peace when our goals and achievements are realized in accordance with our values and beliefs.

If your present belief system makes you feel alive and vibrant, happy and fulfilled, value it. You are blessed! If instead it is making you tormented and confused, it is time for reevaluation.

There is no point in holding on to cobwebs of archaic creeds if they are not enhancing your quality of life. Just because you were taught something as a child does not mean it is correct. There has been a generation or two of new knowledge and understanding since your childhood. The world is constantly changing. Old truths go, new truths come. This age requires us to keep an open mind, review, revise, and readjust our thinking patterns. It's not easy to give up long-held beliefs.

For the sake of happiness and fulfillment, more important than the inherent truth of our belief system is how well it provides meaning to our life. No matter what your belief system, be kind and treat everyone with respect and universal love. *Behavior is more important than belief.*

Certainty in our personal truth should not prevent us from keeping an open mind. Let's continuously grow in our acquisition of knowledge, experience, and wisdom.

If you have the interest and motivation, consider learning more about scientific explanations, philosophies, and the world's religions. Depending on how much time you have, you may read in depth or just skim over for a general overview. The more knowledge we acquire, the more tolerant we become. Having an understanding of varied people's religious viewpoints makes us more accepting. Increased international migration and improved transportation and communication constantly expose us to people with varied cultures and beliefs. We benefit by awakening our consciousness of planetary unity.

There are multiple divisions and varied views within each belief. As an example, some Hindus are atheists, others monotheists, and the majority polytheists. Take time to enjoy the learning process. You have the rest of your life to keep learning. My most fascinating studies began *after* I completed my formal education.

The following are some recommendations on expanding one's understanding of world religions, philosophies, and science. I have provided a brief description of each as an overview, with the realization that there are as many ways of interpreting and *experiencing* any belief system as there are people in this world. Once you have the overview you may learn about them more thoroughly at your leisure. Consider attending gatherings and ceremonies to feel and have the experience, rather than exclusively relying on factual knowledge. Many ceremonies use chanting, dance, or other methods to induce a spiritual or trance-like state.

Hinduism is considered to be the oldest religion in the world. It was founded about 2000 BCE in India. Hinduism is difficult to define because it has no common creed. It has a concept of a supreme spirit, Brahman, and a triad of three chief gods: Brahma, the creator; Vishnu, the preserver; and Shiva, the destroyer. An important element of Hinduism is the social caste system. A Hindu is born into a *caste*. Life is a meaningless cycle of birth and rebirth *(reincarnation)* determined by one's moral behavior in a previous phase of existence *(karma)*. The goal of many Hindus is to reach Nirvana by improving their karma, or by escaping reincarnation by pure acts, thought, and devotion. The sacred writings are many. Recommended are the *Bhagavad-Gita* and *Upanishads*.

Judaism was founded about 1300 BCE and is strictly monotheistic. God is the creator and absolute ruler of the universe and established a particular relationship with the Hebrew people. By obeying the divine law God gave them, they would be a special witness to His mercy and justice. The emphasis in Judaism is on ethical behavior and the true worship of God. Recommended readings include the *Hebrew Bible* (known as the *Old Testament* by Christians). The *Torah* is composed of its first five books which contain the history, laws, and guide to life for correct behavior. The *Talmud* is the collection of writings constituting Jewish civil and religious laws.

Buddhism was founded about 500 BCE near Benares, India. The Buddha is regarded as one of a series of enlightened beings. Buddhism is generally an atheistic religion which rejects the Hindu caste system. Buddhism is predominantly practiced in Thailand, Myanmar (Burma), Nepal, China, Korea, and Japan. Many Buddhists believe that life is misery and decay, and there is no ultimate reality in it or behind it. The cycle of endless birth and rebirth continues because of craving, desire, and attachment to the 'self.' The 'self' is not regarded as permanent; therefore the aim of the Buddhist is to break the chain of *karma,* achieving dissociation from the body. This dissociation is achieved by attaining *Nirvana* (the eradication of all desires) through absorption of the 'self' in the infinite. This aspect of Buddhism is similar to Hinduism. Nirvana can be reached by following the Noble Eight Fold Way: right view, right intention, right speech, right action, right livelihood, right effort, right concentration, right ecstasy. Writings include the *Pitakas* (baskets) and date from second to sixth century ACE. There is also a vast written body of teachings, commentaries, and interpretations. *Zen* is the form of Buddhism brought to Japan in the twelfth century. *Lamaism* began around the eighth century and is the form of Buddhism practiced in Tibet.

Christianity, founded in the second half of the first century ACE, is based on the life of Jesus of Nazareth. Christians believe in monotheism, that the Bible is inspired by God (fundamentalists believe that every word was chosen by God), that Jesus has the power to forgive sins now, and shall return to pass final judgment on the world. Jesus was an incarnation of the one God worshiped by the Jews. Through his life, death, and resurrection, God's revelation became historically tangible. The aim of many Christians is to love others, with the hope of going to heaven after death, where God and his angels live. The sacred texts are the *Old* and *New Testaments.* Read two of the four gospels; *Mark* and *John* are good options. (*Matthew* and *Luke* are thought to have been based on *Mark.*) The gospels were written about 70-100 ACE. Read also at least one of Paul's letters. *I Corinthians* is a good choice. Try a Bible written in modern English. One possibility is *The New Revised Standard Version.*

Islam was founded in 622 ACE in the Arabian peninsula by Mohammed. Islam means 'submission to the will of Allah.' Muslims (believers in Islam) accept an omnipotent, just, and merciful God, the creator of the universe. God's highest creation is man, although man is limited and commits sins. Man is misled by Satan, an evil spirit. God revealed the *Koran* (the sacred writing) to Mohammed to guide men to the truth. Good deeds will be rewarded at the Last Judgment in paradise. Two major divisions of Islam are the *Shiites* who practice in Iran and southern Iraq, and the *Sunnis* who practice in Saudi Arabia and many other middle eastern countries.

The above are considered the five major world religions, many with followers in the hundreds of millions each. The following are examples of religions with fewer followers:

Shintoism is a principal religion of Japan that emphasizes worship and empathetic oneness with nature and ancestors. Traditional Shinto followers stressed obedience and devotion to the emperor. After the Second World War, Shintoism was disestablished as Japan's state religion. Emperor Hirohito disavowed his divinity in 1946.

Taoism is a Chinese religion and philosophy based on the doctrines of Lao-Tse (sixth century BCE). Taoism advocates simplicity and harmonious interaction with the environment. This automatically ensures right behavior.

Jainism, developed in the sixth century BCE, resembles Buddhism. Jainism emphasizes asceticism, sympathy, compassion, and reverence for all living things, including insects and plants. Some wealthy Jainists hire servants to sweep the path in front of them while they are walking, so that they do not accidentally step on insects. Like Buddhism, Jainism is mostly atheistic.

Sikhism is a Hindu sect founded about 1500 in northern India. Sikhs believe in one God, who has never been incarnate in any form, and reject the cast system and idolatry. Sikh men take the last name *Singh* (meaning lion); women take the name *Kaur* (princess).

Bahaism, a modern faith which began in Iran in the middle of the 1800's, teaches the unity of mankind and stresses universal brotherhood and social equality, regardless of religion, race, and gender.

A good book which compares the mythologies of various religions and cultures is *The Power of Myth*. Bill Moyers interviews the late mythologist Joseph Campbell. I enjoyed reading chapters two, six, and eight. The following are some interesting philosophical ideas:

Animism, in religious theory, is the conception of a spiritual reality behind the material one. The soul is independent of the body. Anthropologically, it is a belief of mostly primitive societies that natural objects, such as rocks, seas, mountains, are the abode of dead spirits and gods.

Atheism is the doctrine that there is no God. Atheists think the burden of proof for the existence of God rests on the believer. Furthermore, they point out that everyone is born an atheist and each child learns about gods, ghosts, saints, and demons from their cultural environment. This accounts for the variety of beliefs held by different cultures. *Agnosticism* signifies that one cannot know whether God exists or not. Bertrand Russell (1872-1970), the British philosopher, and Robert Ingersoll (1833-99), an American lawyer and lecturer, are some thinkers who have written on these topics. Russell wrote *Why I am not a Christian.*

Epicurus (340-270 BCE) taught a pleasantly casual school of philosophy in his garden at Athens known as *Epicureanism.* Epicurus found the secret of the good life in the intelligent pursuit of pleasure. Postponing pleasure gratification sometimes leads to more long-term happiness (studying hard for an exam rather than going to a beer guzzling party). Gaining maximum happiness requires wisdom and self-control. Sensual indulgence, if carried to excess, defeats its own ends. The most lasting happiness is found in a quiet life of moderate indulgence and mental activity, amongst pleasant companions, and far removed from the ambitions, worries, and hazards of public life. Epicureanism was a self-centered philosophy, tolerating no emotion strong enough to disturb the serene detachment of the happy sage.

Existentialism is a philosophical and literary movement stemming from Soren Kierkegaard (1813-55), and developed further by Jean-Paul Sartre (1905-80) and Albert Camus (1913-60). It holds that humans are totally free and responsible for their acts, and that this responsibility is the source of the dread and anguish that encompass them.

Humans are the sole judges of their own actions. According to Sartre, people's awareness of their freedom causes anxiety. Therefore they attempt to flee from this awareness into what he calls 'Bad Faith.' Existentialism proposes that humans are nothing more than what they make of themselves.

Humanism dates back to Confucius in China and was also practiced by some of the Greek philosophers. Ignored during the Dark Ages, Humanism resurfaced toward the end of the Middle Ages– the fourteenth and fifteenth centuries. This period was accompanied by fresh attitudes that were represented at successive times by the Renaissance, the Reformation, and the struggle for democracy. These attitudes included release from ecclesiastical authority, liberation of the intellect, faith in progress, and the belief that men and women can apply reason and science to the understanding of the universe and improve their own conditions without supernatural help. Indeed, they have a duty to do so. All individuals have the right and responsibility to think for themselves and to determine their own moral and ethical values. The necessity for humans to show respect to other humans irrespective of class, race, sex, and creed is fundamental to the humanist attitude to life. Among the essential moral principles are those of freedom, justice, tolerance, and happiness. Humanists pride themselves on combining rational and scientific methods with compassion and wisdom.

Pragmatism is a typically American school of philosophy, very practical, started by William James (1842-1910) and Charles Pierce (1831-1914). Pragmatics believe that the validity of beliefs and truths depend not necessarily on their correctness, but on their end result– how well they work.

Utilitarianism is a school of moral philosophy whose proponents were John Stuart Mill (1806-73) and Jeremy Bentham (1748-1832). Utilitarianists believe that the purpose of all action, and society, should be to bring about the greatest happiness to the greatest numbers. This view is based on the premise that all human beings seek to attain pleasure and avoid pain.

Scientific Materialism is another way of understanding the world. Existence may be conceived as a purely biochemical and physical phenomenon, undergoing continuous evolution. According to this view, matter is the only reality; everything in the world, including thoughts and feelings, can be fully explained in terms of interacting atoms and molecules. Consciousness is understood as the interactive product of large sets of neurons. The mind is a product of the physical brain and cannot exist without it. Scientists who hold this view do not believe in God, spirits, or ghosts.

Some scientists who view the world from this perspective also see themselves as humanists. Scientific humanists have lived throughout history. The founder of modern *scientific humanism* was Thomas Huxley (1825-95), grandfather of Aldous Huxley.

Extropianism is a recent development of scientific materialism. As an optimistic *transhumanist* philosophy of life, it applies reason, science, and individual self-determination in seeking to overcome traditional limits to human possibility. Extropians stress the principle of dynamic optimism in their personal lives. They seek to use technology with creative and critical thinking to extend their lifespan, boost their intelligence, increase their freedom, and eventually to expand into space.

While developing our personal truth, it is significant that we remember the following: our personal truth should not interfere with other people's rights. Let's not impose our brand of ethics or morality on those who have a different perspective. Show tolerance and respect to those who have different beliefs as long as theirs do not interfere with your rights. Have a flexible truth that can adapt as you change, grow, and mature. Avoid being dogmatic; don't claim that you, and only you, have all the answers.

Wisdom comes from multiple sources. You don't have to rely exclusively on any one established belief system if none completely satisfy your craving for truth. Some people enjoy creating their own, adding a dash of this, a teaspoon of that, a scoop of another to brew their own personal recipe. We live in a free country, everyone is entitled to develop their own comforting viewpoint.

While hiking through Redwood National Park in northern California, I began to wonder. The redwoods grow to fantastic heights in this region due to the proper mix of ocean-tempered air and healthy soil. A palm tree prefers sandy soil. A mangrove tree prefers swamps. Each species of tree finds its own niche on this planet that suits it best. Each tree within a particular species also grows and adapts differently than its neighbors depending on the particular location its seeds sprout. Locations differ in their degree of healthy soil, amount of sunshine, and wind. It is the same with humans. Each of us has a different genetic code (seed), and we each grow in a different environment. We adapt to this environment by developing our own private truth that works best for our unique situation.

Do not underestimate your potential to self-educate and rationally observe the world the way it presents itself to your eyes. Come to your own awareness about its nature. Keep an open and flexible mind– constantly adapt to your changing environment. Use the full potential of your brain; it has powerful abilities. Its efficiency improves with use. The answers to many of your questions may be nearer than you think.

You can make a difference, perhaps a big difference

If you feel you can have a more meaningful life by actively contributing to this world– curbing violence, family planning to limit overpopulation, nature conservation, improving human rights and education– then join a local political party, run for office, become a member of a school board or local city council, or become involved in positive-goaled organizations. Find a cause to believe in and connect. You can choose the degree of involvement or commitment that best suits your unique self.

An important point to keep in mind is not to feel compelled to sacrifice your health or exhaust yourself in order to save others. You can be of no benefit to society if you yourself become debilitated.

A word of caution about getting involved in organizations and politics: be patient, relaxed, and serene. Get along with everybody, even if they hold drastically different viewpoints. Things change slowly. Overnight miracles are infrequent. Setbacks can happen.

The improvement of society will in turn positively influence our own happiness. Emanate happy and loving ripples that grow, spread... and return.

The mind-body connection

Our thoughts and emotions are associated with the release of brain chemicals and hormones that can enter every cell of our body. Similarly, the body releases hormones and substances that have the ability to enter brain cells, directly influence the formation of neurotransmitters, and alter our moods.

In addition to the bloodstream, the brain and body communicate through four major pathways (all are two-way communications).

1. *The hormonal system*– The brain contains the pituitary gland that secretes various hormones affecting many of our organs such as the adrenals, kidneys, ovaries, testicles, and thyroid. A perception of stress by the brain (a boss yelling) is relayed to the pituitary gland. *Adrenocorticotrophic hormone* (ACTH), one of the hormones released by the pituitary, seeps into the bloodstream, goes to the adrenal gland (located above the kidney) to stimulate the release of adrenaline and cortisol. Adrenaline causes a rapid heart beat, sweating, and heavy breathing.

The brain also has a gland called the *pineal* which is involved with regulating sleep. It does so by secreting melatonin in the evenings. Chronic stress causes sleep disturbances since the release of melatonin by the pineal gland is disturbed. This has profound influences on health since melatonin has the ability to enter and affect the DNA of almost every cell of our body.

Our bodily organs in turn release hormones that enter brain cells. Cortisol, released by the adrenal gland as a consequence of stress, crosses the blood-brain barrier, enters brain nerve cells, goes directly to the DNA, and modifies the production of brain chemicals. Depression is a consequence of chronic cortisol release. Cushing's disease is an illness where the adrenal gland secretes large amounts of cortisol. Patients with this illness often are depressed and have psychiatric disturbances.

Thyroid and ovarian gland malfunction is known to produce mood changes. Low levels of thyroxine cause fatigue. Decreased levels of estrogen production by the ovaries during menopause leads to moods swings in many women.

2. The neural communication between the brain and body is accomplished through the *somatic nervous system* (SNS) and the *autonomic nervous system* (ANS). SNS nerves start in the brain and go down to different levels of the spinal cord where they connect to other nerves *(efferent)* that exit from the spinal cord and supply tendons, muscles and skin. Our thoughts and emotions lead to behavior, that is, the movement of muscles. Movement of facial muscles leads to facial expressions. Muscles move bones except for facial muscles that move skin only.

Incoming *(afferent)* information comes toward the spinal cord or the brain from the sense organs, skin, and muscles. Just as our thoughts and emotions determine behavior, our behavior in turn influences our thoughts and emotions. Behaving angrily leads to more anger; behaving depressed leads to more sadness; smiling and acting happy enhances mood. This is why 'smile' stickers placed around the house and workplace remind us to be cheerful. Some performers are aware of the fact that acting influences mood. One actress reported that acting in a violent role in a movie led to her being more aggressive in her social life; she even hit some people. This was out of character for her.

Positive sensory input stimulate pleasure chemicals in our brain. Aromatherapy and pleasant odors stimulate the brain through the sense of smell; music through the acoustic nerve leads to endorphin release; fine food through taste; scenery, nature, and art through visual system.

The movement, stimulation, or stretching of muscles and nerves elevates mood. There are innumerable ways this is accomplished. Acupuncturists stimulate nerve endings with their needles which transmit information back to the brain, releasing neurotransmitters. Chiropractors manipulate the spine for better alignment and improved neural communication between the brain and the rest of bodily nerves. Massage, yoga, reflexology, Alexander technique, Feldenkrais movement, exercise, Rolfing, and shiatsu (acupressure) also have their mood elevating effects through relaxation or stimulation of nerves of the SNS and the ANS.

3. The ANS is the primary control system– mostly unconscious or involuntary– for our organs and glands such as heart, lungs, thymus, blood vessels, intestines, genitals, kidneys, and skin. (The skin has both somatic and autonomic nerve connections.) The ANS influences heart rate, breathing, digestion, blood pressure, immune system, bowel and urinary function. The emotion of fear stimulates the ANS and thus increase heart rate, sweating, and breathing rate.

Our organs also feed back to the brain by neural pathways. Constipation disturbs mood through distention of the bowels. This information is relayed back to the brain through the ANS. A smile can be the natural outcome from a successful visit to the bathroom. Meditation, visualization, biofeedback, and hypnosis are some of the approaches that influence the function of the ANS, and the immune system.

4. The immune system (IS) is influenced by our thoughts and emotions; and vice versa. The field of *Psychoneuroimmunology* studies this interaction. The brain and the IS are in constant communication. Immune cells in the bloodstream and tissues *(neutrophils, lymphocytes, macrophages, etc.)* have receptors for brain chemicals and brain hormones. For instance, there are serotonin receptors on platelets and white blood cells. Positive moods such as mature love or calm serenity are believed to enhance the IS while negative moods such as chronic anger or bitterness weaken it. Watching a film that induces positive emotions such as joy or love increases antibody levels in the bloodstream within minutes. Anger– genuine or acted– interferes with immunity. Stress disrupts the normal functioning of the IS. Those who are chronically depressed are slightly more likely to get cancer. (Most cancers are not caused by the mind, but the mental realm does play a role in an individual's susceptibility.) Mental depres-

sion decreases the number of white blood cells called *lymphocytes*. There is a special subgroup of lymphocytes called natural killer cells. They circulate throughout the blood, seep into tissues and neutralize any abnormal cells that are on their way to turning into a cancer. The reduced number of natural killer cells makes it more likely for a cancer to get a foothold and start growing.

While fighting off an infection, the immune system releases chemicals that enter the brain and have the potential to interfere with neurotransmitters and alter our moods. Those with a serious infection often get depressed.

I have discussed the four brain-body communication pathways separately, but they are all interrelated. They all interact with each other. For instance, the immune system is in a dynamic state of flux. It influences and is in turn influenced by the brain, the endocrine system, the SNS, and the ANS.

The mind-body communication is a result of extremely complex interactions of countless hormones, peptides, neurotransmitters, amino acids, proteins, minerals, vitamins, lipids, enzymes, cells, etc. I wonder sometimes if we'll ever fully understand all the interactions. The more I learn the details, the more amazed I am of the complexities.

Are the mind and the brain identical? Many scientists now believe that the mind and the brain are one and the same. Consciousness, thoughts, and emotions are due exclusively to the electrical and chemical functions of the brain. The mind cannot exist without the physical brain. Philosophers call this the *mon*istic viewpoint. Other scientists don't fully accept this conclusion. Although they wholeheartedly agree that the mind is dependent upon the physical brain, they feel that there's an additional intangible aspect to the mind, call it *soul, spirit,* or *life force* that cannot be explained by physical means. This is the *dual*istic viewpoint.

A person can lead a fulfilling life accepting either viewpoint.

Natural supplements that improve mood

There are numerous natural substances that influence neurotransmitters, and thus our mood. Their effect is usually not as dramatic as pharmaceutical medicines. Nevertheless, many people notice benefits from using them. It is difficult to give precise dosages and recommend how often to take them since every person has a different chemistry. An additional complicating factor is that different manufacturers make products that have different amounts of the active ingredients. A good approach is to start with a low dose and gradually increase the dose until an effect is noticed. You many also combine low doses of two or more supplements to find the combination that works best for you. Another approach is to use one substance for a few weeks then switch to another. All these supplements appear to safe but no long-term human studies have been done. If you intend to use them for long periods of time, occasionally take a break and don't take them for a few days or few weeks. Consult a physician or nutritionist knowledgeable about these supplements before using them, especially if you have a medical problem or are on medicines. Let's discuss a few of these natural substances.

DMAE or dimethylaminoethanol is present in some seafood. It helps the brain synthesize acetylcholine, a neurotransmitter involved in memory and learning. DMAE has a mood and energy elevating effect. It may take a few days to notice the full effects. DMAE usually comes in the bitartrate form. A pill containing 351 mg of DMAE bitartrate contains 130 mg of pure DMAE. You may start with a quarter pill each morning and gradually increase to half a pill or more. Large doses may induce tenseness in muscles.

Ginkgo Biloba is an extract from the leaves of a tree with the same name. The ginkgo tree has been around for over 100 million years and is the oldest tree species on earth. Apparently it contains substances that has made it adapt well to our planet. Extracts from the leaves of the ginkgo tree have been used therapeutically for millennia. Ginkgo, like ginseng, is mentioned in the traditional Chinese pharmacopoeia. European doctors, especially German and French, write over 10 million prescriptions per year to treat poor circulation. Ginkgo has antioxidant properties due to its flavonoid content. It also improves blood flow to the brain, improves neural transmission, and prevents platelet aggregation on arterial walls. Many users note mood and energy enhancement along with clearer thinking. Dosage: 40 mg of the 24% extract, 50:1 concentration. You may try a dose or two in the morning and possibly another dose or two midday.

Ginseng has been used for thousands of years in the Orient. It contains a group of chemicals known as saponins that can influence brain chemicals such as acetylcholine and serotonin. Many notice improved mood, more energy and physical stamina, and better ability to adapt to stress. Some studies show that ginseng boosts immunity and inhibits some forms of cancer. There are various formulations of ginseng, each with different ingredients and amounts. Try different products to see which work best for you. Dosage is 500 to 1000 mg in the morning. Overuse may lead to nervousness.

Phenylalanine (the L isomer) is an essential amino acid that can be converted to norepinephrine and dopamine. It is available usually as 500 mg capsules. A portion of a capsule (open it and pour out ¼ or ⅓ into a glass of water or juice) in the morning before breakfast leads to alertness and more energy. A high dose may lead to anxiety, nervousness, heart irregularities, and insomnia. Some women find supplementation to be effective in treating premenstrual syndrome and menopausal symptoms. Phenylalanine can raise blood pressure and therefore should not be taken by those who have hypertension or heart disease, or are taking monoamine oxidase type A antidepressants. Phenylketonurics, of course, should not take phenylalanine.

Tyrosine is not an essential amino acid since it can be made from phenylalanine. It is similarly converted in the brain to norepinephrine and dopamine. Tyrosine is effective in improving adaptation to stress. It is available usually as 500 mg capsules. The dosage and effects are similar to phenylalanine. It should also be taken early in the day.

Vitamin B complex supplements can also provide a mild energy boosting and mood enhancing effect. There is a great variety of B complex formulations available. A good rule of thumb is to take pills that have at least 10 mg of thiamin. Take a pill in the morning and possibly another in the early afternoon.

An objective look at mood-improving medicines (more ways to be happier through chemistry)
You've done everything suggested in this book but you're still not feeling your best. You explore other options. You try a few months lying back on your psychoanalyst's couch, your head resting on a comfortable pillow. There's help, but you could use more. You try behavioral therapy and cognitive therapy. Again you note some help but you're still not back to normal. You search other options. You try aromatherapy, hypnotherapy, homeopathy, astrology, numerology, colon hydrotherapy, Celestine prophecy, tarot readings, alien abduction, rebirthing, acupuncture, tantric orgasms, fire walking, primal screaming, bungee jumping, near-death experience, and more. You've met many interesting people and your feel better (except for a slight light-headedness from the bungee dive). The 'giant within' has awakened but is still groggy. What next?

You probably have low, difficult-to-budge levels of brain chemicals (neurotransmitters). This may have been due to genetics (not everyone is born with the same brain chemistry) or due to childhood and adult hardships. Years of leading an unhealthy lifestyle may have also been a contributing factor. There is hope. Human intelligence has created medicines that can help us when nothing else seems to work. These medicines raise the levels of neurotransmitters. They can help you get out of your rut. Just as a diabetic needs additional insulin because of the inadequate amounts made by the pancreas, a patient who has a low mood needs medicines to raise brain chemicals. Take a look back at page seven. As you can see from the diagram, happiness influences every aspect of life. If medicines improve mood, the result is a positive impact on relationships, work, finances, personality, and practically everything else.

"I don't want to talk, I just want a prescription for Prozac," was the first thing a new patient voiced as soon as I walked in the examining room. I looked at the chart handed to me by the nurse. Marjorie, a 42 year old newspaper editor, married with one child, a twelve year old daughter. She continued, "I've read Dr. Kramer's *Listening to Prozac* and I know that Prozac is what I need."

She looked so tense, her upper and lower jaws almost grinding together. Stern-faced, she was menacing. I sat down and tried to elicit a medical and psychological history. Her answers were brief and almost rude. She did not have any past medical or mental problems. Her job was stressful, a boss repeatedly pressured her to have projects ready by unreasonable deadlines, and she was having constant arguments with her husband. She was not in the least interested in discussing any cognitive, behavioral, or other therapeutic options as treatment. After a physical exam including a neurological check-up, and making sure that she did not have any suicidal or homicidal thoughts, I started her on 10 mg of Prozac and prescribed 21 pills.

Three weeks later she was back in the office. I apprehensively walked in the room expecting the stern face. "Hello, Doctor, how's your day going?" she said, flashing a smile. I looked at the chart to make sure she was really Marjorie. "You seem so different," I blurted. She nodded, "I feel calmer than I have for years."

Millions of Americans are using mood-improving prescription medicines. Many have noted significant help. Our moods are associated with the levels and balance of certain mood chemicals in the brain such as serotonin, norepinephrine, dopamine, and phenylethylamine. Low levels of serotonin are implicated in depression, alcohol abuse, low willpower, obsessive-compulsive disorder, bulimia nervosa, and more. Prozac and its cousins Zoloft and Paxil are called selective serotonin reuptake inhibitors (SSRIs). (The word selective is used since they primarily raise serotonin levels as opposed to other brain chemicals.) They prevent serotonin from being broken down by enzymes, thus increasing the amount and time serotonin can influence brain cell receptors. A receptor is a tiny area on the cell membrane of a neuron that a brain chemical can attach to and influence the neuron's function.

What is so different about Prozac and the other SSRIs? Before the SSRIs came on the market other effective antidepressants, such as imipramine and amitryptyline, were available. These antidepressants also elevated brain chemical levels but at a cost. They stimulated many other types of receptors in the brain that were not involved with mood.

Stimulation of receptors such as cholinergic, histaminergic, and adrenergic resulted in many unpleasant side effects thus limiting the use of these medicines to those who were seriously depressed. Newer antidepressants such as Prozac (first available in the US in 1988) have fewer side effects. A new era in psychopharmacology has started. Now even those who are mildly depressed may use these medicines for mood enhancement without 'paying the piper.'

The SSRIs are not totally free of side effects. In higher doses they can cause nausea, dry mouth, impotence, insomnia, and rash. A few years ago there was a media scare about higher rates of suicide in those who had started taking Prozac. Careful studies disproved these claims. It turns out that Prozac does not lead to any more frequent cases of suicide than does placebo or other antidepressants. However, we don't know the long-term effects of these medicines. There are receptors for serotonin not only in our brain, but on certain cells of our immune system such as white blood cells. As of yet we do not know if taking SSRIs for prolonged periods will enhance, interfere, or have little effect on our immune system.

Any form of therapy can have side effects. (Not treating a person who is depressed can sometimes lead him or her to commit suicide. A depressed person also influences the mood of those around them.) Sometimes we overlook the fact that a non-drug treatment, such as psychotherapy, or other alternative methods, can also have side effects if the therapist is not competent. On occasion, a patient may get even more depressed— and commit suicide— if many repressed traumatic emotions are exposed too quickly. The benefits of each type of treatment— or no treatment— versus the possibility of side effects must be carefully weighed. Furthermore, each person is unique and requires a unique approach to treatment.

The discovery of these new medicines and their low side effect profile has blurred the *black or white* way of thinking and treating depression. Many people are beginning to accept the possibility that mood-improving medicines can be used effectively not only in the severely depressed, but also in those who are mildly depressed. Many psychiatrists are using medicines, psychotherapy, and other forms of therapy synergistically, reducing the time it takes to improve a patient's mood. (There is no reason that one form of therapy should prevent the simultaneous use of another form of therapy.) Mild personality trait weaknesses such as low self-esteem have been successfully treated with SSRIs. Recently, some researchers are raising the possibility that even relatively content individuals can take medicines to become even happier.

All drugs, including aspirin, are tools. Aspirin can be used in small doses as an effective blood thinner reducing the risk of heart attacks, or it can lead to stomach ulcers if overdosed. Alcohol can have a health benefit if drunk in small or moderate amounts, yet can be toxic when consumed in large quantities. Similarly, mood-improving medicines can be improperly used (too high doses, for too long) leading to unpleasant side effects or they can be taken appropriately to improve quality of life.

Let's take a look at some medicines human intelligence has discovered over the past few years and that are available to the general public.

Prozac (fluoxetine), Zoloft (sertraline), and Paxil (paroxetine) are SSRIs. This means that they allow serotonin to stay longer in synapses. There are many types of serotonin receptors, such as types 1A, 1B, 1C, 2A, 2B, 3, etc. Different neurons in various parts of the brain have different types of receptors. Serotonin has a different effect depending on which type of neuron is stimulated. For instance, Buspar (buspirone), an anti-anxiety medicine, stimulates neurons with the type 1A receptor. It has a calming effect. Ondansetron is presently marketed as an anti-nausea medicine. It blocks type 3 serotonin receptors. Since the presently available SSRIs elevate serotonin levels everywhere, they stimulate all neurons that have all types of serotonin receptors. Thus, in addition to mood elevation, some unpleasant effects are possible. Side effects are more common with high doses. Few or no side effects are noticed on low doses.

Individuals who have benefited from SSRIs note cheerfulness, enhanced social interactiveness, additional energy, and improved self-esteem. Altering levels of neurotransmitters does change some aspects of personality. SSRIs have been successful in enhancing self-esteem and self-guidance. The three SSRIs mentioned above are not completely similar in their effects. Each of them provides a slightly different type of mood enhancement.

Prozac is available as 10 and 20 mg capsules and liquid solution of 20 mg per teaspoon. Zoloft is available as 50 and 100 mg tablets. Paxil comes in 20 and 30 mg tablets. It's best to start with a quarter or half a pill, using the lowest effective dose. Sometimes it takes a month or so before the full beneficial effects are noticed. Since we don't know the long-term effects of these medicines, it's advisable to slowly taper them and stop after a few months. They can always be restarted again if necessary.

Deprenyl (selegiline is the generic name and Eldepryl is the product name) is a medicine that is primarily used for patients who have Parkinson's disease, a neurological disorder characterized by tremor and muscular rigidity. A small area of the brain, called the substantia nigra, begins to lose its ability to make dopamine. Deprenyl shows great promise not only as a mood-enhancer, but as an intelligence booster and possibly an anti-aging medicine. Middle-aged laboratory mice have lived longer when given deprenyl. People with Parkinson's disease taking deprenyl have lived longer. It has not yet been approved by the FDA as an anti-depressant but studies are ongoing in relation to its mood enhancing effects. There is an enzyme in neuronal synapses called MAO-B (monoamine oxidase type B) which breaks down dopamine, phenylethylamine, and possibly other neurotransmitters. (It is interesting to note that phenylethylamine is one of the neurotransmitters suspected to be involved in the euphoric high experienced during romance.) Deprenyl attaches itself to the MAO-B enzyme and keeps it occupied. This allows mood neurotransmitters to stay in synapses longer and enthusiastically stimulate neurons more. As we age, the activity of MAO-B increases. Thus, older people are especially likely to benefit from this medicine.

When taken in the morning, deprenyl can provide a day-long, continuous, pleasant, mild, nice feeling. Music may sound better. Vision may very slightly be sharper, or colors clearer. Some people notice feeling a little more sexual. Others notice a mild empathic feeling. The euphoriant effects are subtle. Not everyone notices these effects. A few hours after taking it you may notice, in a very subtle way, a difficult to describe "all is well, life is good" feeling. Deprenyl is being used by some physicians as an anti-depressant, either alone or combined with a low dose of an SSRI. Dosage: deprenyl comes in 5 mg tablets. Your physician may wish to start you on a quarter, third, or half a pill early in the morning. It may be used anywhere from once a week to a few times a week. Taking more than 2.5 mg may cause insomnia or jitteriness in the young, although older people may need much higher doses. In one study up to 60 mg was used in depressed patients who had failed to improve on other antidepressants. Some of these difficult to treat patients got better.

Effexor (venlafaxine) came on the market in March of 1994. It elevates both serotonin and norepinephrine levels. Its mood-improving effects may be noticed sooner than the SSRIs. Tablets are available in a range of 25 to 100 mg.

Back to Marjorie. During her second visit she reported having slight insomnia and mild nausea off and on. You recall she was on 10 mg of Prozac a day. I lowered her dose to 5 mg a day, in the liquid form. She returned a month later indicating that she was still getting benefits from the medicine with few if any side effects. Her relationships with her husband and daughter had improved. "My daughter told me 'Mom, you're not yelling at me as much anymore,'" she related. The stress at work was still there, but it was more tolerable. During her third visit she showed interest in combining other forms of therapy. We discussed exercise, a better diet, some attitude changes, and many of the other suggestions that I have written in this book. She continued on Prozac for another four months and then I gradually tapered her off the medicine. I saw her a month after her last dose and she reported that the calmness she had experienced on Prozac had partly faded away but she had incorporated some new coping skills. She preferred to wait and see and continue trying exercise, and other natural methods before restarting the medicine. "I feel comforted to know that a medicine is there for me in case I ever need it again."

The One-Minute *Happiness Quiz*

Circle a number in each category. The higher, the truer.

I have a healthy personality with high self-esteem, strong willpower, and a positive attitude.	1	2	3	4	5
I feel connected and have loving relationships with family, pets, friends, spouse, or lover.	1	2	3	4	5
Old or new emotional wounds have been healed. I harbor little or no hurts, anger, or grudges.	1	2	3	4	5
I have meaningful goals that I'm passionately pursuing.	1	2	3	4	5
Work (and/or school) is satisfying.	1	2	3	4	5
I am financially secure.	1	2	3	4	5
I have many interests and pleasures.	1	2	3	4	5
I am physically healthy. I exercise, sleep well, eat well, and have low stress.	1	2	3	4	5
I enjoy learning and acquiring knowledge. Furthermore, I use my creative talents.	1	2	3	4	5
I have a personal truth or belief system that provides a meaning to my life.	1	2	3	4	5

Score: Total _____

see next page to interpret your score

Quiz Interpretation

10   Double your Prozac dose.

11-25   There's room for improvement.

26-35   Very good. You can learn to be even happier.

36-45   Excellent. You are way beyond the norm.

46-49   Congratulations! Consider writing your own book on happiness.

50   Incredible! Hold on to something. You may be levitating at any moment.

NOTES AND REFERENCES

*There is no such thing as absolute certainty but there
is assurance sufficient for the purposes of human life.*
John Stuart Mill (1806-1873), English philosopher.

OVERVIEW

Friedman, H S, et al. *Personality, Health, and Longevity*, Current Directions in
Psychological Science, 3:2; 37-41, 1994. Bitter, hostile, suspicious, and frustrated people are more prone to cardiovascular disease and all-cause premature
death. This may be due to sympathetic arousal leading to increased stress on
arteries, changes in lipid metabolism, and platelet aggregation. Increasing evidence suggests that those who progress on the path to self-actualization– have
close, loving relationships, playful sense of humor, concerned with broader
issues of ethics and justice, have positive goals, etc.– will be physically healthier and live longer.

Bertoni-Freddari, C, et al. *Neurobiology of the Aging Brain: Morphological
Alterations at Synaptic Regions*, Arch Geron Ger, 12: 253, 1991. The nervous
system has a great capability to modify its structures in response to different
environmental stimuli. Synaptic junctions and organelles of the neuron's terminal regions are dynamic. Even during aging, neurons retain their adaptive
capacities.

Gispen, W. *Neuronal Plasticity and Function*, Clin Neuropharm, 16S:5-11,
1993.

Black, J, et al. *Usual vs Successful Aging: Some Notes on Experiential
Factors*, Neurobio Aging, 12:325-8, 1991. Weanling and adult animals given
extensive opportunities to learn from each other and from toys in the environment typically produce many new dendritic branches and synaptic connections
in occipital cortex and other brain regions after as little as four days.

See Scientific American, Sept 1992. The issue is devoted to the brain.

Crick. *Soul searching with Francis Crick*, Omni, p46, Feb 1994. Dr. Crick
(of Watson and Crick, Nobel laureates) hypothesizes that 'freewill' may be a
region located near the brain's anterior cyngulate gyrus.

CHAPTER ONE
Weston, S and Siever, L. *Biological Correlates of Personality Disorders,* J Pers dis, 129-48, Spring 1993. Excellent review of neurotransmitter correlates of psychiatric disorders.

See J Clin Psychiatry, Oct 1992. The issue pertains to serotonin and its relation to psychiatric illness. The issue discusses serotonergic neuronal system alterations in depression, the role of serotonin in aggression, impulsivity, suicide, and the efficacy of serotonergic antidepressants in obsessive compulsive disorder.

Newsweek, p37-42, 7 Feb 1994. The article, *Beyond Prozac,* discusses potential uses of drugs to treat various personality traits such as shyness, impulsivity, etc.

See Hollister, L. *New Psychotherapeutic Drugs,* J Clin Psychopharm, 14:50-63, 1994.

Enstrom, J E, et al. *Vitamin C Intake and Mortality Among a Sample of The United States Population,* Epidemiology, 3:194-202, 1992.

On 11 April 1993, the *Los Angeles Times* reported how the US measures up to the rest of the world. Of thirty-nine countries studied, the US came in eighth in overall life satisfaction and happiness. The 'happiest' country was Iceland, followed by Sweden, Netherlands, Denmark, N. Ireland, Norway, and Ireland. Japan came in twenty-first.

Ekman, P and Davidson, R. *Voluntary Smiling Changes Regional Brain Activity,* Psychol Science, 342-5, Sept 1993.

Ekman P. *Facial Expressions of Emotions: New Findings, New Questions,* Psychol Sci, 3:34-8, 1992.

Lee, G, et al. *Hemispheric Specialization for Emotional Expression,* Neuropsych, Neuropsychol Beh Neuro, 3:143-8, 1993.

Hinsz, V and Tomhave, J. *Smile and (Half) the World Smiles with You, Frown and You Frown Alone,* Pers Soc Psych Bull, 17:586-92, 1991. The authors conclude 'when smiles are initiated in a social setting, the smiling may spread by contagion, and with it a better mood among the people in the situation. Assuming such a result occurs, ... one wonders why smiling is not encouraged more in our culture.'

CHAPTER TWO
Orth-Gomer, K, et al. *Lack of Social Support and Incidence of Coronary Heart Disease in Middle-Aged Swedish Men,* Psychosom Med, 55:37-43, 1993. Smoking and lack of social support were found to be the two leading factors for heart disease. The article also reports previous studies showing increased mortality from all causes in subjects with few social ties.

Seeman, T E, et al. *Social Ties and Support and Neuroendocrine Function: The MacArthur Studies of Successful Aging*, Annals Beh Med, 16;2:95-105, 1994.

Silverstone, P. *Low Self-Esteem in Different Psychiatric Conditions*, Br J Clin Psych, 30:185-8, 1991. Self-esteem is defined as *the sense of contentment and self-acceptance that stems from a person's appraisal of their own worth, attractiveness, competence, and ability to satisfy their aspirations.* Low self-esteem was found in almost all psychiatric patients, especially those who were depressed, or had personality or eating disorders. Low self-esteem may be the final common pathway of factors causing vulnerability to depression and other mental health problems.

Glennon, F and Joseph, S. *Just World Beliefs, Self-Esteem, and Attitudes Towards Homosexuals with AIDS*, Psychol Rep, 72:584-6, 1994. Northern Irish college students with low self-esteem were more likely to have negative attitudes toward homosexuals. People with low self-esteem discriminate against outgroups in order to enhance their own personal self-esteem.

Epstein, S and Feist, G. *Relation Between Self- and Other-Acceptance and its Moderation by Identification*, J Pers Soc Psych, 54:309-15, 1988. Those who have a favorable attitude towards themselves are likelier to have a favorable attitude towards others.

Batson, C, et al. *Where is the Altruism in the Altruistic Personality?* J Pers Soc Psych, 50:212-20, 1986. Those with high self-esteem are more likely to help others.

Barefoot, J, et al. *Suspiciousness, Health, and Mortality: A Follow-up Study of 500 Older Adults*, Psychosom Med 1987; 49:450-7. Older people followed for fifteen years showed individuals with interpersonal attitudes such as 'cynicism,' 'mistrust,' and a negative attitude towards humankind died sooner.

Curtis, R and Miller, K. *Believing Another Likes or Dislikes You: Behaviors Making the Beliefs Come True*, J Pers Soc Psych, 51:284-90, 1986. This article discusses the self-fulfilling prophecy of 'expectancy confirmation.' When subjects are led to believe that another person liked them, they were more willing to be open with that person, agree more, express similarities, and had a more positive tone of voice and general attitude. When subjects were led to believe that another person disliked them, they expressed a negative attitude.

Time Magazine, 15 Feb 1993. *What is Love?* Fascinating article on love's chemistry.

See also Helen Fisher, PhD. *Anatomy of Love*, Ballantine Books, 1994. It's an excellent book on the evolution of human mating.

Dion, KK and Dion KL. *Psychological Individualism and Romantic Love*, J Soc Beh Pers, 6:17-33, 1991. A study of university students found those who had high self-esteem were less likely to experience romantic love. When they did, it was less intense. They took a more playful, detached, noncommittal approach. They were less likely to feel the need for clinging attachment since they did not wish to give up autonomy. Individualists were also less positive in their attitude toward marriage and less opposed to divorce.

O' Donohue, W and Plaud, J. *The Long-Term Habituation of Sexual Arousal in the Human Male,* J Beh Therap Exp Psych, 22:87-96, 1991. Male college volunteers were shown the same erotic videotapes at weekly intervals for the first three weeks; the following three weeks, they were shown a different erotic tape. They became habituated to the repetitive showing of the same tape and were not aroused. When a new tape was shown, they became aroused again. This study replicated previous findings that males habituate quickly to the same sexual stimulus and recover with new stimuli.

Carter, S and Getz, L. *Monogamy and the Prairie Vole,* Scientific Am, June 1993. Hormones, such as oxytocin and vasopressin, are involved in prairie voles forming long-lasting pair bonds. Debra Kleiman, from the National Zoo in Wash, DC found only three percent of mammals to be faithful to one mate in a lifetime. (Monogamy is more common in birds.)

Houston, B and Vavak, C. *Cynical Hostility: Developmental Factors, Psychosocial Correlates, and Health Behaviors,* Health Psychology, 10:9-17, 1991. Hostile people have a lack of self-esteem and negative feelings toward others. This is often due to parental behavior that was overly strict and critical, inconsistent with discipline (sometimes permissive, other times punitive), or lacking of genuine acceptance (or even rejecting).

CHAPTER THREE

Greenburg, M and Stone, A. *Emotional Disclosure About Traumas and Its Relation to Health: Effects of Previous Disclosure and Trauma Severity,* J Pers Soc Psych, 63:75-84, 1992. Health benefits occur when severe traumas are disclosed. Inhibition of thoughts, feelings, and behavior is an active process requiring physiological work. When individuals inhibit their desire to talk or think about traumatic experiences, cumulative stress is placed on the body, resulting in increased vulnerability to stress-related diseases. Immunity improves with disclosure.

Bery, D and Pennebaker, J. *Nonverbal and Verbal Emotional Expression and Health,* Psychother Psychosom, 59:11-19, 1993. In most species, emotional expression is limited to facial display, body movement, gesture, and nonverbal utterances such as screams and cries. Humans have the additional ability to express through language and art. Inhibiting negative emotions is associated with heightened physiological arousal and health related problems. Talking, or venting through writing, art, dance, music, or expression through other nonverbal methods lowers physiological arousal and improves health. The article lists prior studies where subjects who had not disclosed recent or childhood traumatic experiences were likelier to be diagnosed with cancer, high blood pressure, ulcers, and other major and minor illness. When a traumatic event is written out, the mere act of putting it into words changes the memory of it. It evolves from being a diffuse, chaotic emotional experience into a coherent narrative or story, with a beginning, middle and end. Once it's organized, it can be more readily assimilated and set aside. Further inhibition and suppression becomes unnecessary.

Evans, P and Edgerton, N. *Mood States and Minor Illness,* Br J Med Psychol, 65:177-86, 1992. Hostile moods such as anger, skepticism and tension were found more frequently in the four-day period preceding the onset of cold episodes.

Dembroski, T, et al. *Components of Hostility as Predictors of Sudden Death and Myocardial Infarction in the Multiple Risk Factor Intervention Trial,* Psychosom Med, 51:514-22, 1989. Hostility and antagonistic behavior were found to be risk factors for coronary heart disease.

Siegman, A, et al. *The Angry Voice: Its Effects on the Experience of Anger and Cardiovascular Reactivity,* Psychosom Med, 52:631-43, 1993.

Dua, J and Price, I. *Effectiveness of Training in Negative Thought Reduction and Positive Thought Increment in Reducing Thought-Produced Distress,* J Gen Psych, 154:97-109, 1993. When subjects were trained to replace negative thoughts with positive ones, their mood improved.

CHAPTER FOUR
Brunstein, J. *Personal Goals and Subjective Well-Being: A Longitudinal Study,* J Pers Soc Psych, 65:1061-70, 1993. Successful pursuit of goals has an important role in developing and maintaining well-being.

CHAPTER FIVE
Repetti, R. *Short-Term Effects of Occupational Stressors on Daily Mood and Health Complaints,* Health Psychol, 12:125-31, 1993. Job stress plays a significant role in development of physical and mental health problems. Interpersonal conflict or lack of social support at work increase illness, viral infections, injuries, coronary heart disease, elevated blood pressure, stomach problems, anxiety, depression and headaches.

CHAPTER SEVEN
Shin, W. *Self-Actualization and Wilderness Attitudes,* J Soc Beh Pers, 8:241-56, 1993. There's a positive correlation between wilderness experience and self-actualization. Here are some places to escape for solitude or rejuvenation:

Integral Health Center, Route 1, Box 1720, Buckingham, VA 23921, 804. 969. 3121. Eastern and western yoga, vegetarian meals.

Kripalu Center for Yoga and Health, Box 793, Lenox, MA 02140, 800. 967. 3577. Vegetarian. Yoga and meditation.

New Camaldoli Hermitage, Big Sur, CA 93920, 408. 667. 2456, Benedictine monastery; quiet and contemplative.

Lama Foundation, Box 240 San Cristobal, New Mexico 87564, 505. 586. 1269. Near Taos; spiritual development, ecology, vision quest, dance, and wilderness trips.

Esalen Institute, Big Sur, CA 93920, 408. 667. 3000. Personal growth workshops; massage on a cliff overlooking the Pacific Ocean.

Tassajara Zen Mountain Retreat, Carmel Valley, CA. 415.431.3771. Vegetarian meals, meditation, natural hot baths. Quiet...

For low cost travel and youth hostel information, call *American Youth Hostels at* 202. 783. 6161.

CHAPTER EIGHT

Jacobs, M. *Diet, Nutrition, and Cancer Research: An Overview,* Nutr Today, 19-23, May/ June 1993. Diet is linked to an estimated thirty- five percent of cancer deaths.

Weisburger, J. *Nutritional Approach to Cancer Prevention with Emphasis on Vitamins, Antioxidants, and Carotenoids,* Am J Clin Nutr, 53S:226-37, 1991. Regular intake of fruits and vegetables appreciably lowers the risk of cancer.

Sasaki, S, et al. *An Ecological Study of the Relationship Between Dietary Fat Intake and Breast Cancer Mortality,* Prev Med, 22:187-202, 1993. Data from thirty countries found a positive association between dietary fat and breast cancer mortality.

Coyle, T and Puttfarcken, P. *Oxidative Stress, Glutamate, and Neurodegenerative Disorders,* Science, 29, 689-695 Oct 1993.

Masoro, E. *Retardation of Aging Processes by Food Restriction: An Experimental Tool,* Am J Clin Nutr, 55S:1250-2, 1992.

Idrobo, F, et al. *Dietary Restriction: Effects on Radial Maze Learning and Lipofuscin Pigment Deposition in the Hippocampus and Frontal Cortex,* Arch Geron Ger, 6:355-62, 1987.

Lee, I, et al. *Body Weight and Mortality,* JAMA, 23:2823-8, 15 Dec 1993.

Williamson, D and Pamuk, E. *The Association Between Weight Loss and Increased Longevity,* Ann Int Med, 119:731-6, 1993.

Kuller, L and Wing, R. *Weight Loss and Mortality,* Ann Int Med, 119:630-3, 1993. There have been reports that loss of weight over a lifetime actually decreases lifespan. The authors caution us to interpret these studies carefully.

The studies did not determine whether weight loss was voluntary or due to illness. Furthermore, smokers may be more likely than non-smokers to lose weight. The authors believe that slow weight loss over time improves health and reduces risk from diabetes, hypertension, and heart disease.

Johnson, L E. *The Emerging Role of Vitamins as Antioxidants*, Arch Fam Med, 3 September, 1994, 809-18. Excellent review of latest antioxidant studies.

Hemila, H. *Vitamin C and the Common Cold*, Br J Nutr, 67:3-16, 1992. Excellent review.

Block, G. *Vitamin C and Cancer Prevention: The Epidemiologic Evidence,* Am J Clin Nutr, 53S:270-82, 1991.

Gerster, H. *Anticarcinogenic Effect of Common Carotenoids,* Int J Nutr Res, 63:93-121, 1993. Excellent review.

Gerster, H. *Potential Role of Beta-Carotene in the Prevention of Cardiovascular Disease,* Int J Vit Nutr Res, 61:277-91, 1991.

Hunter, D, et al. *A Prospective Study of the Intake of Vitamins C, E, and A and the Risk of Breast Cancer,* NEJM, 329:234-40, 22 July 1993. Women in the top 20% of dietary vitamin A intake have less breast cancer than women in the lowest 20%.

Knekt, P, et al. *Vitamin E and Cancer Prevention,* Am J Clin Nutr, 53S:283-6, 1991.

Stamper, M, et al. *Vitamin E Consumption and the Risk of Coronary Disease in Women,* NEJM, 1444, 20 May 1993.

Vitale, S, et al. *Plasma Antioxidants and Risk of Cortical and Nuclear Cataract,* Epidem, 195-203, May 1993. Those with high levels of serum vitamin E had a lower incidence of nuclear cataract.

Hallfrisch, J and Muller, C. *Does Diet Provide Adequate Amounts of Calcium, Iron, Magnesium, and Zinc in a Well-Educated Adult Population?* Exper Gerent, 28:473-83, 1993. Half of this educated population consumed less than two-thirds of the RDA. Therefore, supplementation with minerals may be helpful.

Lindsted, K, et al. *Coffee Consumption and Cause-Specific Mortality,* J Clin Epidem, 45:733-42, 1992. Heavy coffee consumption leads to a slight increase in heart disease and mortality.

Mitsuoka, T. *Intestinal Flora and Aging,* Nutr Rev, 438-46, Dec 1992. Excellent review.

De Simone, C, et al. *The Role of Probiotics in Modulation of the Immune System in Man and Animals,* Int J Immunother, 1:23-8, 1993.

Simopoulos, A. *Omega-3 Fatty Acids in Health and Disease and in Growth and Development,* Am J Clin Nutr, 54:438-63, 1991.

Drevon, C. *Marine Oils and their Effects,* Nutr Rev, 38-45, April 1992.

Irwin, M, et al. *Electroencephalographic Sleep and Natural Killer Activity in Depressed Patients and Control Subjects,* Psychos Med, 54:10-21, 1992. Both depression and insomnia caused a reduction in natural killer cells.

Sack, R and Lewy, A. *Human Circadian Rhythms: Lessons from the Blind,* Ann Med, 25:303-5, 1993.

Hardeland, R, et al. *The Significance of the Metabolism of the Neurohormone Melatonin: Antioxidative Protection and Formation of Bioactive Substances.* Neuroscience Biobeh Rev, 17:347-357, 1993. "Melatonin is the most potent physiological scavenger of hydroxyl radicals found to date," and may protect from cancer.

Saarela, S and Reiter, R. *Function of Melatonin in Thermoregulatory Processes,* Life Sciences, 54:295-311, 1993.

Kloeden, P, et al. *Timekeeping in Genetically Programmed Aging,* Exp Ger, 28:109-118, 1993.

Haimov, I, et al. *Sleep Disorders and Melatonin Rhythms in Elderly People,* Brit Med J, 309:167, 1994.

Miller, T and Miller, D. *Dreaming: The Impact of Life Stress Events,* Psychiatric Develop, 4:367-373, 1989. Excellent article.

Wu, K and Lam, D. *The Relationship Between Daily Stress and Health: Replicating and Extending Previous Findings,* Psychol Health, 8:329-44, 1993.

Cohen, S, et al. *Negative Life Events, Perceived Stress, Negative Affect, and Susceptibility to Colds,* J Pers Soc Psych, 64: 131-40, 1993.

Herbert, TB and Cohen, S. *Stress and Immunity in Humans: A Meta-Analytic Review,* Psychosom Med, 55:364-79, 1993. Stress decreases the response to antigens, natural killer cell activity, circulating white blood cells, immunoglobulin levels, and antibody titers to herpes virus.

Leonard, B. *Stress, the Immune System and Psychiatric Illness,* Stress Med, 4:207-13, 1988. Immune function abnormalities release substances that cross the blood-brain barrier and cause psychiatric illness.

Green, M, et al. *Daily Relaxation Modifies Serum and Salivary Immunoglobulins and Psychophysiologic Symptom Severity,* Biofeedback Self-Regulation, 13:187-99, 1988. After a session of relaxation, IgA in saliva was significantly higher in the subjects than in the control. After three weeks of daily training in relaxation, the immunoglobulin was even higher.

McGinnis, J, et al. *Actual Causes of Death in the United States,* JAMA, 2207-12, 10 Nov 1993.

Ear plugs: If you can't find them in local stores, call 3M Corporation at 1.800.328.1667 for a supplier near you. Buy a box of 200 pairs; this will last many years.

CHAPTER TEN

The 11 Oct 1993 Time magazine article, *How Did Life Begin?*, discusses an April 1993 experiment at Scripps Research Institute in La Jolla, California. In 1953, Stanley Miller, a University of Chicago graduate student, created amino acids when electrical sparks (substituting lightning) went through a glass jar containing water, methane, ammonia and hydrogen. Scientists have since believed that this is how the components of protein and life began. Now, scientists believe that RNA, a genetic master molecule, preceded proteins. Gerald Joyce, from Scripps, found synthetic RNA in his test tube. Within an hour of its formation, it began to replicate itself. The article also discusses the possibility that organic material may have come to earth on comets, asteroids, and meteorites, and that life could have sprouted on earth many times before taking a permanent foothold.

For information about *Extropy* institute, call 310.398.0375.

APPENDIX

Kropiunigg, U. *Basics in Psychoneuroimmunology,* Ann Med, 25:473-9, 1993. *Psychoneuroimmunology* studies direct two-way connection and communication between the mind and body. The central nervous system influences the immune system through the *hypothalamic pituitary adrenal axis,* sending nerves to almost all lymphatic tissues including the thymus, bronchus-associated lymphoid tissue, spleen, and tonsil. In turn, substances from the immune system such as *thymosin peptides, interleukins,* and *interferons* enter the brain, influencing release of neurotransmitters and neuropeptides.

Zachariae, R, et al. *Changes in Cellular Immune Function After Immune Specific Guided Imagery and Relaxation in High and Low Hypnotizable Healthy Subjects,* Psychother Psychosom, 61:74-92, 1994. Guided imagery and relaxation cause changes in the immune system.

Hiramoto, R, et al. *Identification of Specific Pathways of Communication Between the CNS and NK Cell System,* Life Sci, 53:527-40, 1993. Central nervous and immune systems are in constant communication. Immune cells have receptors for neurotransmitters.

Solomon, G. *Whither Psychoneuroimmunology? A New Era of Immunology, of Psychosomatic Medicine, and of Neuroscience,* Brain Beh Imm, 7:352-366, 1993. Excellent historical review.

See also the Spring 1993 issue of Advances, *The J of Mind-Body Health.* The issue has a great discussion on the relationship of mind (brain) and body as it relates to the immune system.

Crick, F and Koch, C. *The Problem of Consciousness,* Scientific Am, Sep 1992. "Most neuroscientists now believe that all aspects of mind, including its most puzzling attribute– consciousness or awareness– are likely to be explainable in a more materialistic way as the behavior of large sets of interacting neurons."

Klenjnen, J and Knipschild, P. *Ginkgo Biloba,* Lancet, 7:1136-39, Nov 1992.

Tollefson, G D, et al. *Absence of a Relationship Between Adverse Events and Suicidality During Pharmacotherapy for Depression,* J Clin Psychopharm, 14:163-9, 1991.

Knoll, J. *The Pharmacological Basis of the Beneficial Effects of Deprenyl in Parkinson's and Alzheimer's Diseases,* J Neural Transm, 40S: 69-91, 1993.

INDEX